Lorna Livey

Two Journeys

Swimming from Darkness to Light

Lorna Livey

MOORE HOUSE

Miami   Toronto

National Library of Canada Cataloguing in Publication Data

Livey, Lorna 1951-

Two journeys: swimming from darkness to light

ISBN 978-0-9916734-0-7

This work is a memoir. Some names and identifying details have been changed. Dialogue and events have been recreated from memory.

Illustrations: Lorna Livey www.lornalivey.com
Book design: Andrew Livey
Cover design: Nicole Schaeffer
Cover photography: Gregory Edwards

Dedicated to Holly Hicks Hanson
April 28, 1921 - September 21, 2012

To my mom with gratitude for her love
and support and for inspiring a passion
for travel and reading.

Alter Ego, Etching, 4" x 6", 2012

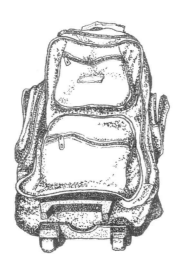

CHAPTER ONE

"A life safety device has been triggered in this area. We are investigating the cause. Please listen for further updates."

This was a decidedly unpropitious start of my late mid-life crisis.

The announcement alternated with an alarm of incessant, teeth-rattling beeping followed by two sweet notes from what sounded like a glockenspiel. The other passengers in the departure lounge were ignoring both the ominous sounding alarm and the announcement. Perhaps they didn't understand either the English or French version or was it simply a matter of having heard it too often while waiting in similar departure lounges—the equivalent of "crying wolf"?

To my right, a woman in a puffy jacket almost touched heads with a slightly-built Asian man as they conferred over a Blackberry.

"Tell her we're at the airport," said the young man.

"Yeah," she replied. "Flying to China to meet the new in-laws."

They looked way too young to be married. A honeymoon in Asia—how exotic.

August 27, 1972

"Okay, you take the bow and I'll do the stern. We'll have to flip it to carry it to the water," John said as he reached the end of the upturned canoe. It was lashed to the roof of the car that was on loan from my father.

As I scraped my end of the canoe across the wooden car-top rails, I silently cursed our decision to save money on our honeymoon by using the ancient fiberglass canoe that had been at his family's cottage for years rather than rent a lightweight aluminum one. It was a short distance to the water, and we were able to drag rather than carry the weighty vessel to the edge of the lake.

The canoe route in Mississagi Provincial Park that we chose was a series of small lakes joined by varying length portages, culminating in a downstream paddle on the Mississagi River. Never having done a canoe trip together, we optimistically estimated that it would take four days to complete.

We were finally launched, the canoe low in the water with its heavy load, and I struggled to keep pace with John's more confident paddle strokes.

"Dip it in as far as you can go. That's right, keep your lower hand close to the gunnels," he said.

My hand painfully made contact with the splintery cedar gunnels. Eventually, I mastered the stroke well enough not to splash him every time I lifted the paddle out of the water.

Our plan for portaging was to do a two-person carry of the heavy canoe on the first trip, returning back over the portage to lug all our camping gear and supplies. At the first portage—after many false starts—we managed to coordinate our lifting techniques to maneuver the canoe onto our shoulders.

"Start walking," John said.

"Where?" My muffled voice came from the innards of the upside-down canoe. All I could see were my sandals, which were sinking in the boggy shore. The canoe jerked forward and hit the low branch of a tree.

"Not that way," he yelled. "Follow the path."

"What path?" I asked. Rather than a cleared smooth trail, there was only a steep uneven expanse of rock beneath me.

"Back up," I said. "I think the canoe is crushing me."

It seemed the only way to portage the canoe was for John to carry it alone while I walked ahead with some of our gear trying to find the easiest route and shouting navigational instructions back to him. Teamwork it was, but not the teamwork we envisioned when planning our trip.

Later that afternoon, exhausted by paddling and carrying the canoe and overloaded packs, we decided to lighten our load for the next day by drinking the bottle of sparkling wine that was to have celebrated the mid-point of our honeymoon adventure. John paddled out to a deep spot in the lake, tied the wine bottle securely to a rope and lowered it into the water. He reached for his fishing rod, and as the wine cooled, he cast his lure hoping to catch some fish for dinner. Fishless, but with a lovely cold bottle of wine, he paddled back to our campsite. He aimed the bottle towards the lake, and the stopper arced out over the silver smooth water creating a ripple of perfect concentric circles as it hit. We raised our tin cups.

"To my beautiful wife," John said as our cups clanked together.

Before crawling into our tiny tent, we suspended our food pack high in the air between two trees to keep it out of reach of wild animals, particularly bears. Relaxed by the wine and exhausted by the day's exertions, we were asleep almost immediately.

"Scritch, scritch."

"What's that noise?" I whispered to my sleeping mate. I wondered what animal could be pawing at our tent. Now fully awake, I could tell that the noises were coming from all over the outside of the tent.

"They're trying to get in!" I poked harder at my new husband's shoulder.

He opened his eyes, looked up at the roof of the tent and said, "It's only mice." He turned away from me in our shared sleeping bag.

I checked that the tent's zipper was fully closed, leaving no mouse gaps at the ground, and finally fell asleep.

Morning brought confirmation that mice had taken over the camping site. They were capable tightrope walkers, and had managed to infiltrate the suspended food bag where they devoured the cheesecake I'd lovingly prepared from an expensive dehydrated food kit.

Eating proved to be a challenge. Swarms of mosquitoes descended on us whenever we stopped to prepare a meal. We wore strange head gear and lifted up the edge of the netting long enough to shovel food into our mouths and snap the elastic edge back in place. Occasionally, a mosquito managed to make it under the net and into our mouths along with the Kraft Dinner. The macaroni and cheese powder in a box was a staple in our camping diet because it was relatively light to carry, cheap and filling.

It was our last day. We were packing the canoe at the end of the final portage, our load lightened by having eaten most of the contents of the food pack. We were looking forward to a leisurely end to our trip, floating downriver with no portages.

A couple burst from the portage we had just finished. The man was easily carrying a canoe, and he was followed by a woman jogging with a substantial pack on her shoulders.

"Hey," the man said. "We thought we were the only ones on this route. No one else to share our honeymoon." He smiled at his young bride.

"It was an easy two day trip," she said, looking like she hadn't broken a sweat.

John and I looked at one another. It had taken us four long and arduous days—lake after lake, portage after portage, and one mosquito/mouse plagued day after another. We may not have finished the trail in two days, but maybe the challenges of our honeymoon prepared us for nineteen years of marriage.

John took his second wife to Paris for their honeymoon.

The alarm startled me as it sounded again. I rummaged through the pocket of my carry-on bag looking for the chocolate bar purchased earlier in the Duty Free Shop. A little comfort food should quell my nervousness. I read the Nutrition Facts on the wrapper. Three squares of dark chocolate contained one hundred and eighty calories, a small price to pay for its calming effects. I hoped the sugar and caffeine in the chocolate wouldn't keep me awake on the sixteen-hour flight. The alarm finally stopped without any updates on why it had been triggered, and I relaxed, my tensed shoulders dropping back to their normal position.

I was in the almost deserted airport at eleven at night waiting for a flight to Taipei, Taiwan, and then a connecting flight to Bali, Indonesia. I was turning sixty, and this milestone birthday marked—in my mind—the transition from middle-age to old-age. My descent into the sunset years had gained speed when I became a grandmother. Recently, I had given a speech at the opening of a senior's art exhibition. I looked out at a room full of white or sparsely haired heads and deeply etched faces and realized I was soon to join their ranks.

Now I was embarking on what was to me the ultimate escape—a month-long solo journey to Bali. Escaping Canada's brutal February cold and darkness was an obvious reason for this trip. It was a way to seek sun, light and heat in an exotic and remote destination. I had made many such journeys seeking warmth and light but never to Bali, never for so long and never alone.

February 5, 2007

Bitterly cold weather, one degree, negative thirteen degrees with the wind chill. Hard to keep building heated. Gas fireplace kept the chilblains away as I sewed the pillow covers. Put heater in rental apartment hoping to thaw it before the young girl comes to look at it. Even the pens are frozen. Discouraged by lack of a renter, no loss of weight and general February malaise. Trying to stay committed to writing and sketching for potential book/portfolio—especially when I go away. Travels and adventures with baby boomer neurotic artist. So cold it's hard to keep out of bed where the fat duvet insulates against both cold and life. Apartment bone-chilling fifty-eight degrees on rising, up to balmy sixty-five degrees by noon.

The pierced nose, short, tight jacket, hood lined with fake fur—scant use against the bitter cold. The boyfriend with tough guy toque. Both impressed by the concept of an airy perched bed in the tiny loft space; the better to leave the room below free for partying. Their blind optimism about the concept of traveling on public transit. The boy's naiveté in asking about the personal safety of his girlfriend.

My choice—the innocent waif with nose piercing or the confident swagger of the tongue-pierced, rather large black woman who has also applied to rent the apartment. Mother to one, what to the other?

I needed to lighten my mind and body of daily responsibilities, those of family—an elderly mother, needy children and infant grandchildren—and work: landlady, teacher, master printmaker and self-employed artist. Traveling was a way for me to find meaning as a single woman, independent from my family. By immersing myself in a radically different culture, I hoped to prove my self-sufficiency. Also I needed time to think about why I always screwed up my relationships with men.

I winced as I bent over to replace the chocolate bar in the carry-on bag at my feet. I had hoped this trip would help break my addiction to dark chocolate. I wasn't doing well on that front. Putting it out of sight might prevent me from devouring the whole thing only two hours into my trip.

A fall earlier in the day had triggered the pain in my back. I was skating with my son Andrew and two-year-old granddaughter Ava, and as we were leaving the ice, my feet shot up in front of me. I took the full weight of my body on one cheek of my buttock. I am well padded there, but as I was falling, it flashed through my head that I might break an arm, a leg or a hip on the day I was flying to Bali.

"Are you alright, Ma?" Andrew asked as he helped me to my feet.

"I'll live," I said.

Now, as I put the chocolate away at Departure Gate 57, I regretted having further strained my back by vacuuming and cleaning my apartment in a frenzied pre-trip attack on dust bunnies and disorder. I knew stretching my spine would ease the pain, so I bent over pretending to be looking for something in my bag. I didn't want to look like an ostrich with my head between my legs, like someone about to pass out.

I needn't have worried. My fellow passengers were paying as little attention to me as they had paid to the earlier incessant alarm.

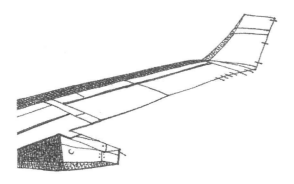

CHAPTER TWO

I had booked my flight online with Eva Air. The fare was the cheapest I could find, and the only stop en route was Taipei. None of my friends had ever heard of the airline, but I confirmed it existed by checking the airline boards at the entrance to the airport on an earlier trip. I joined the company's Evergreen Club, and was impressed with their service when I received a preflight information email a few days before leaving.

After I boarded the plane, I saw that the Evergreen theme determined the color of nearly everything on board including the upholstery on the seats. The plastic tray containing our first meal was an interesting shade of pale lime green as was the plastic cutlery and the tray's paper placemat. The cutlery was substantial, not the easily bent and broken white plastic stuff. I stashed my unused spoon in my purse in case of an emergency situation requiring a spoon.

The seatback video screen provided information on several cities in Asia and Europe where Eva Air flew. Since we were heading for Taipei and I would be staying there on my return trip, I checked what was written about that city. The English translation presented intriguing images. It informed me that "Yangmingsan Park is regarded as the rear garden of Taipei City." The flower festival held there celebrated "the blossom of cherry, cuckoo, and also all kinds of flower." In the section on cuisine, it exalted the virtues of "stinking tofu." The recipe for stinking tofu is "to dry up fresh tofu, then mixed with a lot of seasoning and preserved for a period of time to stink. Stinking tofu is somehow like French blue cheese, smell stink but taste delicious." Since I loved blue cheese, I could seek out "stinking tofu" when I was in Taipei on my return trip.

This is fun, I thought. What do they say about other cities? I scrolled down the list and clicked on Vienna. I read about "a typical coffeehouse, where you will find all kinds of newpaper and even the poll table, serves a cup of coffee with a silver plate and a cup of water holding a spoon facing down." I puzzled over the images being presented and sympathized with the writer who had struggled with the language.

Flying west, the night started with a dinner at two in the morning, Toronto time. Then the lights were dimmed, and I tried to sleep. At around seven in the morning, a flight attendant offered those of us who were still awake a bun containing mystery meat and cheese. Outside, the almost-full moon shone brilliantly. Then it was twelve noon Toronto time, and the moon continued to pierce the inky black void. The reflection of the moon on the wing added a soft secondary glow, like that of a nightlight. How long would this night last? It was a quarter to three in the afternoon and it was still dark. The night-without-end offered the opportunity to sleep for a long time, but sleeping upright had always been a challenge for me.

Since sleep seemed out of the question, I began socializing with my seatmates, who were also not sleeping.

"Are you staying in Taipei?" I asked the man beside me. He might know where to find the stinking tofu.

"No, I'm flying on to Ho Chi Ming City to visit my sister," he replied in a soft voice so as to not disturb the people who appeared to be sleeping.

"What about you?" I asked the middle-aged woman in the aisle seat.

"I'm traveling to Manila to see my mother. I go home every two years. Who are you going to visit?"

"No one," I replied cheerfully. "I'm going to spend a month in Bali by myself."

My seatmates exchanged doubtful looks as though they couldn't understand traveling so far, for so long, for no practical reason

Breakfast arrived on a green tray at three in the afternoon Toronto time, and with a spirit of adventure I chose the Chinese congee over the less exotic omelet. The congee was flavorful, topped with small pieces of chicken and green onion snippets. A side dish held what could have been half a duck egg—at least I'd like to think it was duck—accompanied by salty, crunchy seaweed tied in a bow knot. This was my first taste on this trip of real Asian cuisine, as much as any airplane food can be described as real.

CHAPTER THREE

The time between flights on long journeys feels like being condemned to purgatory. Taipei airport was different. I felt like Alice falling down the rabbit's hole. First, I saw free internet computers, and I was able to report home that all was well. Then, I discovered all sorts of funky attractions to visit. The first one was the Hello Kitty Baby Nursing Station with a Hello Kitty public phone beside the room. This seemed to be the birthplace of Hello Kitty because I found a Hello Kitty play area, a Hello Kitty nursery and a whole huge store devoted to Hello Kitty merchandise with the young female sales staff all dressed in identical pink pinafores. There was even a Hello Kitty departure gate where grown men sat on Hello Kitty embellished pink moulded plastic chairs.

There were other themed departure gates including the Postal Service lounge, the Thomas the Train lounge and the Aboriginal Peoples lounge. My grandchildren, Griffin and Ava, would love this place.

My favorite area was a Green Relaxing Zone with potted plants and trees and large poster boards laminated with huge photos of indigenous plants and insects. The best part of the Green Relaxing Zone was the free massage chair activated by tokens available at a store nearby.

I deposited a token, sat down and marveled as the chair moved into a reclining position. Unexpectedly, the leg rests started to close and squeeze my calves as the head rest began to ripple and undulate, massaging the muscles in my neck. At first I panicked. This machine had taken my body captive, and I feared my calves might never be released from the squeezing grip of the black padded leather. I was barely able to turn my head, caught as it was in the clutches of the perpetual motion chair, but I was able to move it enough to see that the man in the chair beside me didn't look as panicked as I felt.

Gradually, I relaxed to the rhythm of the squeezes and noticed the sounds of chirping birds and insects. I closed my eyes and could almost imagine that I was being caressed by strong masculine hands in a tropical paradise. Perhaps this was a foretaste of what was to come in Bali.

My second most pleasurable discovery was an orchid garden. I hadn't known that the phalaenopsis orchid was the official flower of Taiwan. My one phalaenopsis orchid at home had bloomed just two days before my trip after failing to bloom for two years. I love drawing orchids and two of my most popular botanical etchings are images of orchids. Hundreds of fuchsia blooms tumbled out of one raised planter while yellow blossoms speckled with blood-red spots spilled from a planter level with the floor.

I was so enthralled by the Taipei Airport that I briefly toyed with the idea of spending my whole month there. Unfortunately, the airport wasn't all fanciful departure lounges, sexy flowers and free massage chairs. I came to the part that made it just like any other large international airport. There were rows and rows of brand name Duty Free stores—Dior, Chanel, Burberry, Lancôme, Godiva, Givency. Each was staffed by attractive young people in uniforms or suits standing guard over the luxury goods. These were not the kind of stores I could afford. Tiny boxes of Godiva chocolates cost sixty dollars. I was relieved I still had some of my three-dollar-and-seventy-five-cent chocolate bar.

Hungry after four hours spent ogling orchids, extricating myself from massage chairs and sightseeing, I found a small refreshment stand. I bought an exotic papaya milk drink served in a domed, transparent plastic cup. Sucking the refreshing drink through a funky turquoise straw with a large bendy section, I considered taking the straw home as a souvenir but realized these straws were probably available in Toronto.

I was enjoying my exploration and thought back to some of my other airport experiences when I wasn't alone. They were memorable for upset stomachs and short tempers. My dad was especially prone to airport anxiety.

"You've packed too much stuff. I bet we'll have to pay extra."

"I told you we needed more time to get to the airport."

"Don't tell me you've lost our passports?"

Subsequently, when I traveled with someone, I worried about every detail, fearing the wrath of my partner should something go wrong, and that if it did, it would be my fault. I thought of the angry words I had written in a journal on a trip to Naples. I was with a boyfriend (a word more appropriate for teenagers) and a married couple who were his friends. I had come across the entry when looking for notebooks to bring with me on this trip.

September 14, 2007

I've learned my lesson. Play dumb, don't have an opinion, don't make any suggestions—they'll be overruled anyway. Don't try to figure out where you are, what direction to go, where and when to eat and drink. Agree with everything. Don't take a leadership role. Be passive, be pleas-

ant no matter what, and laugh at all the jokes even if they're not funny. Don't give cab drivers information. Agree with racism. Respond positively to all comments. Be sure to drink and eat whatever everyone else is having, even when you don't want that much alcohol or food. Dress the way they are dressed. Wear a bra, don't wear a hat. Don't slow everyone down by taking pictures, looking at architecture, sculpture, art or whatever. FIT IN—don't show any independence. Pretend you belong even when you know you don't. Don't look at a guide book or map. Pretend you don't know where you are even if you do know. Don't suggest any form of public transit.

If I screwed up on this solo trip to Bali, the world wouldn't come to an end since I was only responsible for myself.

Chapter Four

As luck would have it, two other airplanes landed at the same time as ours in Bali. One was from Kuala Lumpur, the other from Moscow. We stood in huge untidy lines, first to pay for a visa and then to go through Customs.

Finally through the line, I went to withdraw rupiah, the Balinese currency, from an ATM machine. In my nervousness, I used my VISA card instead of my debit card. An exorbitant rate of interest would likely be charged on that amount until I returned home in a month's time.

Outside the airport, I encountered a semi-circular wall of men holding up signs with the names of people who had prearranged drives to their accommodation. I systematically checked each name going counterclockwise. I needed to be close to read them because I hadn't had time to dig my glasses out of my crammed purse. About ten signs along, I saw my name in an enormous type size. When I had established eye contact with the man holding the sign, I excitedly pointed to myself. I was relieved the arrangements I had made by email from Canada were reliable.

The driver, Made, a slight man in his fifties, was congenial but quiet on the hour drive to Ubud.

"Do you have children?" I asked, trying to draw him into conversation.

"Old children, boy and girl," he replied.

"Just like me," I said, happy to have found some common ground.

"Husband not come to Bali?" I detected a note of reproach in his question.

"I'm divorced. No husband," I replied.

"You need driver for Kuta?" he asked, his tone hopeful.

"No thank you. I'm not going there. Too many tourists. Too many parties."

I wondered why he thought I would want to visit Kuta, which I intentionally decided to avoid because of its reputation as a destination for young Australians looking for a good time. My fantasies of Bali were more of the *Eat, Pray, Love* variety described in Elizabeth Gilbert's book and the movie version. Admittedly, I was no Julia Roberts, and men like Janvier Bardem might prove hard to find in Bali.

It *would* be nice to find the equivalent of Janvier in Bali. Most of my best prospects in the last twenty years were found at singles dances.

July 3, 1992

Things looking up. Movie last night with Brian. Got up the courage tonight to go to Singles Dance at Boulevard Club. Met real gentleman named Stephen. He's been separated 8 months; 2 kids, girl 7 & boy 9. Great physical attraction. We seem a lot alike—both wounded & hurt with fragile self-esteem. Hope he calls. I guess there's life after marriage after all

February 8, 1993

Annoyed at Stephen yesterday. He continues to profess his love for Rose. He's worse than me for flogging a dead horse. He longs for some image of family life that never seems to have existed. Think I should back off. Whenever I want someone, that person backs off. I am not "the object of desire." I am the pursuer, not the pursued and so am not valued. The irony of life—loved by those whose love I don't value enough and scorned by those I love.

My chances of finding a compatible mate seemed to improve when my daughter Alison got me into online dating. She'd found her husband online—even though it had taken fifty *first* dates.

Unfortunately, as in real life, most men on internet dating sites were looking for women younger than themselves. I wanted to think of myself as a "cougar," but maybe older women finding younger men happened only on television. One man who responded to my profile was *Sweetboy522*, a seventy-three-year-old man looking for "a woman with no mixed or gray hair, fit, no baggage and between five foot one and five foot five in height." I met two of his four criteria, but I found it puzzling that a man of his age wouldn't consider as a potential mate a woman who had "mixed" hair.

Michaelrw suggested, as a first date, "supper or luch (sic) or just coffee or whatever you drink Talk about likes and dislikes long walk get to know more about each other may hit a movie if we like each other then go from there see what tomorrow brings." *Michaelrw* obviously had no interest in the nuances of punctuation and capitalization.

The futility of finding a kindred soul and potential partner through the internet was confirmed when I read the profile of *hipmonk788*, who was seventy-two years old.

yes, I am a hopeless case,
then all men are helpless without a good woman as part of his life
men just exist in this world without a good woman to rake care
of him
that makes me normal. Or dose it

i can cook, clean house, and do laundry but my pillow dose not
hug me back

The photograph on his profile showed an unsmiling, round-faced, unshaven man wearing an old fashioned, hand-knit Mary Maxim sweater. The bulkiness of the sweater accentuated rather than camouflaged his substantial beer belly. In the section describing a first date, he wrote,

where, where are you to-night why did you leave me here all alone
i looked the world over and thought i found true love.

you found another and poof you are gone

life is great

Hipmonk788's writing looked like a new style of free-form poetry, but the thoughts he expressed cast a pall of sadness over the whole idea of online dating.

CHAPTER FIVE

The impossibly narrow roads of Bali were jammed with cars, trucks and thousands of motorbikes whose drivers were all claiming the same spot in the road. As we passed through several villages, it became apparent—and was confirmed by Made—that each village was famous for making a different product.

First, there was the furniture village with outdoor workshops jammed right to the edge of the road. The ornately carved wooden furniture had acquired the patina of age from exposure to the weather and from the coating of dust created by a constant stream of traffic.

Next along the route was the sculpture village with hundreds of statues overflowing from the workshops. The statues appeared to have been carved from stone or cast in concrete. Gargoyles kept company with reclining Buddhas, Hindu gods and ornate water fountains.

After the batik village, we passed through the gold and silver village. Finally, four villages later, we arrived at our destination, the town of Ubud, the painting center of Bali. I had chosen it as my initial destination because of its reputation as the cultural heart of the country.

By now, the twenty-seven hour journey, lack of sleep and hot steamy air, combined with the chaos of the roads and the hodge-podge of shops, produced the biggest culture shock I'd ever experienced. Everything around me seemed strange and unreal. I followed Made down a long, walled path, like a labyrinth, to a family compound. The courtyard we walked through had an open-sided temple on a raised platform and several small buildings. This was Jati Homestay, the accommodation I had booked online. The man who checked my name on the hand-written ledger handed me a thin, tiny towel and a small roll of toilet paper minus the cardboard core.

Rustic is probably the best word to describe the room. The furniture was sparse: a bed, a dresser, a bamboo chair and a night table. I was glad to see the mosquito net hanging from the ceiling above the double bed. Later that evening, as I struggled to lower the net, it proved more decorative than functional. To cover both my head and feet, I had to scrunch as far towards the foot of the bed as I could. Once I was enclosed within the net, the translucent fabric felt like a death shroud. I decided to sleep undraped and at the mercy of the mosquitoes. Perhaps I would regret I hadn't had malaria shots prior to this trip.

The bathroom had a set of taps, a shower head and a drain hole at one end and a sink and toilet at the other. That was it. I was glad I had packed soap, shampoo, hair conditioner and a facecloth. A small glass shelf above the sink would hold some of my toiletries, and I hung the towel I had been given on a hook in the wall.

In spite of the starkness of the room, the balcony more than made up for it. The highest branches of a plumeria tree were within touching distance. A few feet beyond the plumeria and a small palm tree was a rice field patterned with rows of tender shoots. The field was about two hundred feet deep, and large trees on the other side screened the view of what lay beyond.

I unpacked most of my clothing into the dresser drawers, which were lined with newspapers and mothballs. I didn't want to use the bottom drawer since it had not been prepared in the same way. It had obviously accommodated a family of mice. I'll let them have one drawer and maybe they'll leave my things alone, I thought. I hoped Balinese mice didn't have the kleptomaniac tendencies of certain Canadian mice.

I looked at the red Samsung vacuum cleaner with distaste. The dirt bag was full. The easiest thing would be to open the lid, pull out the plump paper bag, fasten the self-adhesive strip over the musty, hairy hole and toss it in the garbage. I hesitated. What if my lost black pearl earring was in that mass of dust and cat hair? It was the other contents of that refuse bag that disgusted me. Mouse turds. Copious amounts of them.

Eleven years of living with a cat in my apartment kept it free of mice. The cat, Arthur, never had the opportunity to prove himself as a mouser since his presence alone seemed to do the trick. Arthur had been gone eight months, and with the cool October weather, the mice had moved in. The ironic part was that the food, which kept them well fed, was Arthur's bag of cat kibble. With an optimism grounded in the off-chance Arthur would magically reappear, I kept his food on the bottom shelf of the pantry cupboard. Since I didn't use the cat food, the mice gorged themselves without being discovered.

One day I decided to give Arthur's special treats to a friend for his cats. I made the horrible discovery—an empty and crumbling cat food bag and the "calling cards" left by what seemed like a huge extended family of mice. The mice, well-fed and knowing by instinct that there was no cat, had branched out from the bottom shelf of the pantry. Soon I discovered mouse turds in the overflow of empty plastic yogurt containers and lids on another shelf. Finally, I had a reason to cull the tsunami of yogurt tubs. The mice had even infiltrated piles of tea towels and dishcloths. I washed the linens in hot water and bleach. The harsh chemical ate a few holes in them, but they were purged of the evidence of the unwanted mice.

Thinking back a few months, I realized I had mistaken the source of rustling noises in the ceiling. I heard the sounds as I read in my comfortable Lazyboy chair in the living area and before falling asleep in my bedroom. I thought the noise was from the resident family of raccoons whose younger members regularly partied on my flat roof by sliding down a small domed skylight. The noise was caused, not by raccoons on the roof, but by mice in the ceiling. They were creating cozy nests in the pink fluffy insulation and were copulating lustily.

I needed to reclaim my space. I replaced the tattered cat food bag with fluorescent turquoise poison pellets and laid enticing trails at the edge of the cover hiding the hot water radiator behind my chair. I made generous piles in the space under the low shelf where I kept my supply of wine, booze and obscure liquors. Too bad the mice didn't have an addiction to alcohol rather than cat kibble.

Within a day, the brightly coloured pellets had been replaced with mouse turds. I put out more piles of pellets. Finally, the mice had consumed a whole box, and still the nocturnal rustlings in my ceiling continued. I was afraid to try lifting a ceiling tile in my bedroom to place some poison there, in case a whole family of mice, fibreglass insulation and turds fell on my head, on my bed and on the collection of knick knacks and perfume bottles on my dresser. It was safer to deposit the pellets in my kitchen and living areas and hope the indulgent Mommy and Daddy mice would carry the colorful morsels to their brood.

I tried a new brand of gourmet mouse poison. Paraffin blocks contained enticing nuts and seeds and looked somewhat like nougat bars. I broke the bars into sections about two inches long and one inch in diameter. These new treats didn't interest the mice as much as the turquoise pellets. They stayed in place for three days with only a few nibbled corners, as though the mice were sampling this new offering but hadn't yet decided if it met their culinary standards. Then whole chunks disappeared, a miracle of mousey engineering because the pieces were almost as big as the mice themselves. Had Mommy or Daddy mouse dragged the nut bar up the interior of the walls and across twenty feet of ceiling to feed their family nestled in the comfort of my bedroom ceiling? Maybe those nut bars were feeding a whole neighbourhood of mouse families, a

Thanksgiving feast courtesy of the kind lady who had generously supplied the bag of cat food.

I put out more and more pieces of nut bar. More and more pieces of nut bar disappeared from the pantry shelf, from under the radiator and from under the booze shelf. Rather than debilitating the mice, it seemed to generate more mouse turds and mice rustlings. I began to consider moving, an option more appealing than living with a growing mouse colony.

After a month of feeding the mice, I was startled one morning by a grey lump lying in front of my refrigerator. I inched closer. It was a dead mouse. The package directions on both the turquoise morsels and the paraffin nut bars said nothing about dead mouse bodies. Wasn't the poison supposed to make them die of thirst and their bodies dry up, out of sight and with no odor, in the walls, in the ceiling, anywhere but in front of my refrigerator?

As I considered how to deal with a dead mouse, a slight movement of the grey lump meant I had a completely new problem, how to deal with a not-quite-dead mouse. It was bad enough to pick up a dead body and deposit it in the garbage, but disposing of a live—albeit comatose—mouse was an even greater challenge. How could I dispatch it as humanely as possible? I couldn't stomp on it, the blood and guts would be too gory to stomach. Should I try to put it in a plastic bag and have it suffocate? No, that was a long and lingering death. I contemplated picking it up with a plastic bag the same way one picks up dog poop, but dog poop doesn't move when you pick it up.

I thought of a solution. I'd call a friend. He'd know what to do. As a single divorced woman, I'd always been proud of my self-sufficiency. Home repairs, painting, papering, shoveling and mowing, I did them all. But semi-dead mouse removal, that was a different story. Feeling somewhat sheepish, I called my friend's number and explained the situation. He didn't laugh or belittle me for my distress.

"Use two plastic bags together and pick it up like dog poop," he suggested.

"But it's still alive. I can't pick up a live mouse with only plastic bags between him and me." I had already decided that this was a male mouse, *the big brother from one of the many families populating my ceiling.*

"What if he tries to bite me? Don't mice carry terrible diseases?" I squealed.

"Okay," he replied, "Do you have a dust pan?"

"Of course," I said.

"How about a broom?"

"Yes, I have a dust pan and a broom," I responded with a hint of exasperation in my voice.

"Okay, use the dust pan to scoop up the mouse and keep him in place with the broom. Carry him like that to the bathroom and flush him down the toilet."

I doubted that this was a humane method and that such a big mouse—or worse, a small rat—could be flushed without blocking the toilet. He assured me that flushing was a clean, quick way to die as opposed to my plan of depositing him in the outside garbage can where he was bound to suffer a long and malodorous death. I promised to phone him back when the deed was done.

I grabbed the dust pan and the broom and gingerly approached my nemesis. Trembling, I gently slid the dust pan under the mouse's body. Suddenly, with a great expenditure of strength from his formerly inert body, the mouse jumped off the dust pan. I screamed and thrust the dust pan once again under the mouse and clamped the broom on top to prevent his escaping again. Although his body was covered by the broom, the mouse's tail continued to writhe as I ran screaming to the bathroom. I thrust the dust pan towards the toilet and the mouse fell with a plop that showered me with drops of toilet water. With revulsion, I slammed the lid down and flushed. When the bowl had refilled with water, I peeked under the lid to see whether the mouse was indeed gone or had managed to block the toilet. There was no sign of the mouse, but to make sure it wasn't hiding just out of sight, I flushed the toilet again.

As the weeks progressed, I offered the mouse poison on a rotational basis, turquoise pellets followed by the chunky seed bars. Four more corpses materialized in different locations, but still the poison was consumed. I continued to vacuum up the mouse turds.

Now I was forced to make a decision. The vacuum bag was full. I was missing a black pearl earring that had disappeared during my battle with the mice. I could look for it among the disgusting contents of the bag or I could throw away the bag without ripping it apart. I choose the latter rationalizing that the resourceful mice, grown fat and strong on mouse poison, had acquired a shiny bauble to decorate their mouse metropolis.

CHAPTER SIX

There was a small convenience store at the head of the pathway leading to my homestay. A group of young boys monopolized a bench in front of the store.

As I passed them to go into the store, one spoke up. "Lady, what is your name?"

"Lorna," I replied, "what's yours?"

"Nyoman."

"No-oh-what?" I asked. It was a source of great fun and much giggling among his companions as I attempted to pronounce his name. Once I was successful, they giggled some more, and I entered the store to buy some bottled water and ask for directions to a restaurant.

The clerk in the store couldn't suggest someplace to eat, so I ventured out to track down a place on my own. I passed several open-fronted shops selling clothing, beads and handmade soap. Around the corner, in a narrow laneway, I discovered a simple *warung* or restaurant. The only other people there were the owner/cook/waitress and her son, who was perhaps ten years old, watching a tiny television perched precariously on a tall cupboard. After consulting the menu, which was helpfully accompanied by photographs of the food, I chose a meatball soup and a bottle of cold tea. The tea was in a soda bottle and the soup came steaming hot. It consisted of marble-sized balls of canned spam, noodles and chopped greens similar to swiss chard. The broth was very spicy, and I decided that too much of the fiery liquid would upset my stomach. The meal was simple but filling. I had no idea what I was paying for it because as I held out a bank note the woman took it and then gave me a bunch of bills as change.

My guidebook suggested purchasing a sarong as soon as possible so as to be able to enter any of the thousands of temples located throughout the country. Returning to my homestay on that first evening in Ubud, I passed many shops that were selling sarongs. Fortified by my dinner, I decided to be brave and stopped to browse at one of the shops.

Immediately, a sales girl leapt on me, and I became the victim of a constant harangue. "You like this? Or this? Very good price, very good price."

I prefer to be left alone when I shop, and the pressure of her constant questions made me want to escape. But I did need a sarong. To end my agony, I quickly chose a piece of cloth and asked the price. Looking for an even better sale, she thrust another length of cloth towards me.

"This much better, hand-woven, very nice."

She noticed my hesitation and grabbed others from the rack.

"You no like color. This nice color. I show how to wear."

She skillfully wrapped the fabric around my waist. She reached for an iridescent mother-of-pearl shell cut into the shape of a double loop.

"This very nice. Help keep sarong in place."

With the sarong tied around my waist I realized that I was too far into the ritual to tear it off and flee the shop. By now, we had attracted an audience. The sales girls from the neighboring stores added their own words of encouragement.

"Very nice, very nice."

The sales girl could sense my indecision.

"You buy two or three. Better price. You have mother. You have daughter. Very beautiful sarong."

I knew I couldn't escape and pointed to the first sarong I had touched.

"How much for this one?" It was the second time I had asked the price.

She named her price, one hundred and seventy thousand rupiah, and waited. My travel-addled mind tried to figure out the equivalent amount in American dollars. As a rule of thumb, my Frommers guidebook had recommended equating ten thousand rupiah to one American dollar, and so I figured the asking price for the sarong was less than twenty dollars. I agreed quickly, hoping to end my shopping torment.

I dug into my money belt, retrieving what was left of the rupiah I had withdrawn from the ATM machine at the airport. She looked at it, shook her head with disgust and proceeded to try to teach me the intricacies of Balinese currency. All the zeroes were confusing, and it was then I realized that instead of withdrawing the equivalent of two hundred dollars from the ATM machine at the airport that I had withdrawn only twenty.

Unwilling to miss out on the sale, she asked if I had American money. Taking out a twenty dollar bill, I handed it to her, expecting change in return. She conferred with her fellow sales ladies and asked me to wait while one of them ran to a nearby money changer. She returned with a fistful of bills and handed them to my sales lady. She, in turn, handed me a few rupiah. I'd expected more back. When questioned, she quoted a rate of exchange from the money changer that was much less than the guide book number. I'd just had my first lesson in the hazards of international currency exchanges.

Chapter Seven

That first night I discovered that the scenic charms of being close to a rice field were overrated. As I tried to get to sleep, I was serenaded by a cacophony of frogs, crickets and night birds accompanied by the rustlings of the mice, either in the set of drawers at the foot of my bed or in the bamboo walls. I wasn't thrilled to find out later that the Balinese didn't know what mice were, identifying their particular rodents as rats. The windows had no glass, only screens, and the walls were thin. It was like sleeping in a tent with no barriers to muffle the night sounds. Through the thin bamboo-mat walls, I could hear female voices in the room to my right, but no sounds from the room to my left.

I was exhausted by my trip and finally fell asleep. At about four in the morning, I was woken by the crowing of roosters that sounded loud enough to have been just outside my door. They *were* just outside my door. The roosters were just the prelude to the full chorus, and they were joined at daybreak by more roosters, a soprano section composed of birds, the staccato tenor of dogs and the swishing percussive sound of a broom. Obviously, I wouldn't need the travel alarm I had brought with me, but I *could* make use of the earplugs I'd thrown into my suitcase at the last minute.

After breakfast, I sought out Butu, the stocky young man who had escorted me to my room the previous afternoon. Then, his manner had been lackadaisical and abrupt, probably from being roused from an afternoon nap in a room adjacent to the homestay kitchen. Now, he was more obliging and helpful when I asked for his recommendation of a good place to get a massage. I figured I'd earned this indulgence after my long trip and restless night.

"This very good massage," he said, showing me a brochure he picked up from a nearby table. "I book now for you. Not far. They send driver."

I looked at the brochure. A massage and body exfoliation would help to alleviate my jet lag. Before I had time to change my mind, I was on the back of a scooter. I held on tightly to the tiny waist of the young woman sent by the spa. This was a new experience: risking life and limb on the back of a scooter without the protection of a helmet. I was as scared being a passenger on this type of vehicle as I was eleven years ago.

"There's no way I'm climbing on behind you. If you want me to go on a motorcycle, I drive or there's no deal."

My boyfriend looked disappointed that I was turning down the offer of a ride on his newly restored vintage Yamaha XS 650 motorcycle. He had spent many months rebuilding the engine, having parts rechromed and replacing the cracked black leather on the seat with finely stitched midnight-blue leather. He had pulled up in front of where I lived expecting a different response to the offer of a ride on his gleaming pride and joy.

"I even borrowed my brother's helmet for you." Then, reaching into one of the newly purchased saddlebags, he drew out a battered, black leather motorcycle jacket. "This is for you. I wore it when I bought my first bike. It's too small for me now. The leather must have gotten wet

and shrunk."

He had obviously been much thinner in his youth as it was nowhere close to being large enough to fit his forty-eight-year-old body.

"Just try it on," he urged.

It was a classic bomber jacket, circa 1975. Heavy zippers on three slash pockets and on the bottom of the sleeves matched the front zipper. A thin leather band held in place by loops circled the narrow stand-up collar. Two buckled straps stitched into the side seams and extending to the back cinched in the bottom of the jacket. The leather had a distressed look — the patina of age. It was the type of retro leather jacket I'd always wanted — biker chick, James Dean era.

"It fits," he said, as I slipped on the jacket.

He was right. Other than the length of the sleeves, which he subsequently had shortened for me, the jacket fit perfectly.

"Come on," he said as he thrust the helmet towards me. "We'll only go around the block."

The issue for me was one of trust. Could I hand my safety over to this man I'd been dating seven years? It seemed about time that I took the risk. If not now, then when?

Helmet in place, jacket snugly zipped, I climbed on behind him and clung to his middle-aged "spare tire" as he pulled the machine away from the curb.

For the remaining four years of our turbulent relationship, the custody of the motorcycle jacket passed back and forth between us as our break-ups became more frequent. One day he just walked out of my life, and I was left with final custody of the battered garment.

Safely delivered to the spa by my young female scooter driver, I stood before a receptionist, who softly offered me lemongrass tea in a moss green, fragile ceramic cup. She asked which fragranced body oil I wanted for my massage, showing me four different bottles. I had to decide which exfoliating mixture I would like for my body scrub. Did I want to be invigorated, soothed or refreshed? Did I need an antioxidant, heating, cooling or sensitive skin mixture? My travel-addled brain was still unable to function. I pointed to two random oil and body scrub mixtures. Had I chosen wisely? Maybe the chocolate and coconut mixture would be more invigorating, or perhaps the spice mixture would clear the fog from my brain.

It really didn't matter.

The two-and-a-half-hour-long experience was blissful and painful at the same time. The woman's strong fingers found every knotted muscle in my body. She discovered sore spots I didn't know existed until she started applying direct pressure. After the hour of torture/ pleasure, she applied the exfoliation mixture, first rubbing it into my skin and then roughly rubbing it off again with a coarse cloth. This was followed by a gooey, scented mixture that was made from cucumbers. I was wrapped in a nylon body sheet and allowed to marinate in this fragrant potion.

The thought crossed my mind that I was being prepared as a human sacrifice. First, I was tenderized with oil and then marinated for flavor. I wondered what the next step might be after she scrubbed away the cucumber mixture. She pulled aside a curtain and revealed a black stone soaking tub, the water surface totally covered by golden plumeria flowers and scarlet rose petals. A kumquat juice drink, protected by a leaf, sat beside the tub. If all human sacrifices were treated this well, what a way to go.

The sacrifice wasn't me. It was some of the contents of my money belt. The equivalent of twenty-five dollars that I handed over was worth it. I politely turned down the offer of a ride back and decided to take my chances as a pedestrian on the busy road.

Chapter Eight

A visit to the Ubud Monkey Sanctuary was magical. The sky was overcast, the air hot and steamy. Huge, magnificent trees with hanging roots and vines provided the perfect playground for the resident monkeys. As well as the live variety, there were monkey statues everywhere, some of which were humorous, some lewd and a few a bit of both. The real monkeys were the same. Couples indulged in mutual grooming, obligingly picking bugs off their mates and popping the rewards into their own mouths. One couple was indulging in some "monkey business," and a few bachelors were looking after their own needs. Verdant moss, nurtured by the humid, shaded rainforest, covered many of the temples and the sculptures of grotesque creatures and evil spirits.

As I sat down on a stone step to write in my notebook, I noticed a motion out of the corner of my eye. Isn't that cute? I thought, as a small grey monkey sat down beside me and eyed me companionably.

What he was really eyeing was my purse, which he grabbed, hoping it contained contraband food. I had taken out a bunch of wrapped candies at the ticket booth because signs warned that marauding monkeys would steal your bags or search your pockets if they caught even a whiff of food. Removing the candy didn't guarantee the smell of food was totally gone.

"Mommy, do you have a Kleenex?"

Alison licked at the pink streams of ice cream running down the sides of her cone. Some had already reached her tiny fist clenched around the cone and were dribbling towards her elbow.

Kleenex? I had enough mangy pieces of Kleenex in my purse to create a nest for a whole family of mice.

"Just a minute, sweetheart," I replied. "Mommy's purse has a lot in it."

That was an understatement. I had inherited my dad's frugal habits, especially that of pocketing—or in my case, putting in my purse—any leftover packets of condiments from fast food places. Sugar packets, tiny paper tubes of salt and pepper, cellophane packets of saltine crackers— anything that would have been discarded by the restaurant was fair game.

My purse was also jammed with other essentials: a slot-headed screwdriver, broken bits of wax crayons, penny-saving grocery coupons, a Big Bird figurine dressed as a lifeguard from McDonalds and scraps of used envelopes scrawled with words like milk, bread, apples and toilet paper. I was forever losing my keys in that bottomless pit to the exasperation of my family—especially my husband.

I shoved my hand down into the debris.

"Oh, oh," I said, sparing Alison and Andrew from the not-so-nice word I was thinking. My husband had recently admonished me for using the word starting in "s" and ending in "t" in their presence.

I pulled out a slimy, red mass of clotted Kleenex. Maybe it hadn't been such a good idea to save packages of ketchup from our last fast food lunch.

A tug-of-war ensued between me and the tiny monkey. I wasn't going to sacrifice my purse containing my money, passport, glasses and other essentials. The signs in the sanctuary suggested letting the monkeys win over disputed property. I looked around desperately for a monkey keeper to rescue me and my purse. A gardener, working nearby, hissed at the monkey, startling it. The monkey let go, and I yanked my purse back.

I didn't sit down again while I was in the sanctuary. I wrote standing up, with one eye on the lookout for the greedy creatures.

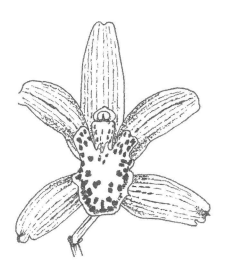

Chapter Nine

I was sitting on a mossy bench, which was carved from a huge root, in the meditation court at the Ubud Botanic Garden. I had started walking early that morning to try to find the garden, not really knowing how far away it was. I was following a road that was mostly uphill through a few small villages where men tried to sell me their taxi services. These services would probably have been on the back of a motorcycle or scooter as I didn't see any cars around. Every once in a while, I would ask women sitting in open-air shops, like miniature convenience stores, if the garden was still ahead. I would say "garden" and point to the road ahead; they would nod their heads and also point to the road ahead. Perhaps they had no idea what I was asking, but they decided the appropriate response was to nod agreement and mimic my pointing. After about an hour, and perhaps three kilometers of walking, I found myself in front of the garden entrance.

I had found the Garden of Eden. Would I be Eve and find my Adam here? There were few visitors, and most of the time I was alone in a steamy, lush, scented rainforest garden. Signs pointed the way along paths paved with small stones set into the earth. In places, there were cement stepping stones embellished with the impression of leaves. In the Islamic Garden, stones arranged in stylized floral patterns paved the circular path. A small river flowed through the garden. I heard only the sound of the river, sometimes accompanied by a chorus of insects and birds. Occasionally, I heard the trumpeting of the ubiquitous roosters.

It felt like a semi-tamed jungle. The lush undergrowth almost obscured the paths. Huge trees towered overhead with vines descending almost to the ground. Thousands of ferns and tropical plants carpeted the jungle floor. There were so many beautiful flowers and richly patterned vegetation to photograph that I panicked about my camera running out of battery power. I saw six different varieties of butterflies flitting through patches of sunlight where the canopy wasn't so dense.

The sign at the entrance to the secluded meditation area said "Silence please." Easy to do; I was alone.

Being alone. That was what I wanted to think about in this quiet place. Would it have been better to share this beauty with another person, specifically a male partner? Would it make it even more meaningful to have a companion in this paradise? It would have to be the *right* man. It needed to be someone who wouldn't have minded the tiring trek here and who would have patiently waited while I took photographs of countless flowers. The perfect partner would have appreciated the verdant beauty of this almost wild place, companionably sharing the silence in this circle.

Maybe a perfect mate didn't exist at this point in my life, and perhaps he would never exist. I was sharing this incredible experience in Bali by writing about it. My notebook was my companion. This writing would probably not have happened if I'd been traveling with a man, so being alone offered an opportunity for reflection, growth and creativity.

By now, the ants had discovered that I was on their bench and the mosquitoes had found skin unprotected by clothing. The seat of my pants was wet from the damp wood of the undulating bench. It was time to make the descent to Ubud.

As I got up, I realized the ants had attacked my body. They were tiny ants, and in my musings on life I didn't notice them crawling up my arms and legs, even into the armholes of my oversize t-shirt. I frantically tried to brush them off, hoping they were not the biting kind but already feeling some tingling on my arms. Then, as I picked up my purse, I realized it was full of ants. I'd left the zipper open to remove my notebook. One of nature's smallest creatures proved to be the greatest hazard to meditating and writing en plein air.

On my return walk from the garden to Ubud, I was joined by a young Swiss woman who was wise in the ways of tropical ants.

"They don't bite," she said. "They pee on you. It's their urine that makes you itch." The idea of being peed on was gross.

"Have a shower as soon as you get to where you're staying or the itching will just get worse, and you'll break out in a rash," she said.

She was traveling alone, and we both agreed it was easier that way to meet other people, both tourists and locals. She told a sad tale of a holiday romance gone awry, and we commiserated on the faults of the opposite sex. As if to confirm this opinion, two young men on motorcycles drew abreast of us and began to hustle "taxi services" at an exorbitant rate.

"Forget it," she told them. "You're thieves."

A young Swiss woman proved to be more assertive than a much older Canadian one. She also knew a lot more about ant pee.

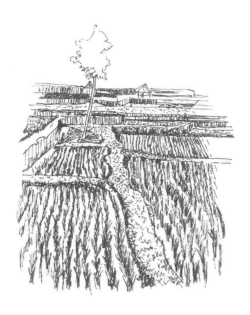

Chapter Ten

One day I decided to get out of the bustling town of Ubud and do a rice field walk. Even with a map and directions from two German men in the room next to mine, I couldn't find the entrance to the rice field walking trail. One route looked promising because it led from the street down a very steep flight of steps to a path beside a river. Rice fields need water, so I assumed that this was the correct route. The path ended abruptly. I huffed back up the slippery stairs—it had poured rain the night before—and asked for directions from a shopkeeper. He pointed me in the right direction and told me what to look for at the entrance to the path. He warned that there was no sign to mark the spot where the path began.

The path was paved with stones, but it soon petered out to a mud trail. The open vistas, fresh air free of traffic exhaust, absence of other people and relative quiet were a welcome change from the chaos of the town. These rice fields were relatively flat, unlike some of the steeply terraced ones shown in the photograph on the cover of my guide book. The walking was easy, and although it was overcast, the conditions were excellent for hiking. I had been warned by the German men at my homestay not to miss the cutoff for the short loop back to town. If I did, I was in for a four-hour hike rather than the hour-and-a-half walk I'd planned. A tiny little bamboo hut that offered snacks was supposed to mark this junction. I reached the hut, but the trail leading to the right that I was told to take looked steep, muddy and not at all like a proper hiking trail. The old man at the hut noticed my confusion, so he took my hand, helped me down the slick, steep incline and pointed to where I should go. Without his help, I doubt I would have made my way back to Ubud and might have wandered indefinitely in the fields.

The narrow path followed a small river in a trough capped by the rice fields. Once out of this green valley, the trail was again level with the fields. The only other person along the path, other than the old man who had led me in the right direction, was a rice farmer with a sideline business. He offered a limited product line: fresh coconut juice. His overhead was low. The coconuts were overhead, a machete was his only tool, and a package of straws was his only expense. Always willing to support a fellow entrepreneur, I accepted his offer of a drink. Within minutes, I was sipping the liquid from its ecologically correct container, the coconut itself.

The quantity of juice in the shell was enormous. Although I didn't want to hurt his feelings by not finishing it, I had to leave some for fear that there was no place along the route where I could relieve my bursting bladder. As I walked away, he called after me and gestured that there was more to come. He used his machete to chop the coconut open. He took a sharp, thin stone out of a plastic bag, thoughtfully rinsed it with the leftover juice and sliced slivers of raw coconut from the shell. The consistency was somewhat slimy but had an interesting flavor, not as coconutty as I expected. Refreshed, I continued my stroll back to Ubud.

My second "raw" food that day was at lunch. The day before, I had checked out a spa and restaurant, called Taksu, located near my homestay. It was a New Age establishment. Although it was very posh and beautiful, the prices for both the spa treatments and the meals were reasonable. I selected the lasagna from the "raw" section of the menu, having never sampled this type of cuisine. The lasagna was served with a "raw side salad," a name I thought was a tad redundant since most salads are raw. The lasagna itself was a surprise. Instead of wheat or rice noodles, the pasta was uncooked zucchini strips layered with cucumber, tomatoes and three types of peppers. I felt nutritionally virtuous eating it.

The spa was located in the valley of a small river with a series of pavilions, meditation spaces and individual treatment rooms situated on either side of the steep valley walls. I was led down one side of the valley, across a cobblestone bridge and back up the other side to my treatment pavilion where Boncel, a tall, slender young man, waited, posing in the doorway at the top of the flight of steps. There seemed to be no other customers anywhere at the spa so I felt pampered and special.

I was to have the *Lomi Lomi Massage*, and the next sixty minutes were blissful. Perhaps "lomi lomi" meant "lovely, lovely" in English. Using mostly his elbows, he kneaded, soothed and caressed my back, shoulders, legs, feet, toes, arms, fingers, stomach, neck and head. The only parts he missed, which were modestly covered by a towel, were my buttocks, pubic area and breasts. I lapsed into a relaxed stupor. The only time he spoke, other than to ask if the pressure he was using was okay, was to say quietly with his hands clasped together in front of his face that the treatment had ended. I considered feigning unconsciousness so I could stay on that padded table forever with the gentle breeze wafting through the curtains.

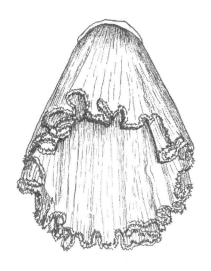

Chapter Eleven

On one of my many walks through Ubud, I stopped to take a photograph of a sign that marked the entrance to usti's Garden Bungalow. Closer inspection of the sign revealed that the letter "G" had fallen off, so this was, in fact, Gusti's Garden Bungalow. Different shrubs covered in multi-hued flowers almost obscured the entrance and the garden wall adjacent to it. The attractive entrance with its ornately carved wooden door, and the prospect of staying in a bungalow surrounded by a garden, tempted me to have a look at the place.

If the price wasn't too high, I could move from my homestay. Jati had its charms, in spite of the mice and roosters, but I didn't feel connected to the place. I had passed many members of the multigenerational family in the long walkways and courtyards on the way to my room. Ten or eleven young children played there and were minded by a tiny, wrinkled-faced woman, who I assumed was their grandmother. Perhaps I had a romantic vision of playing with the children and making some sort of connection with the grandmother, but they mostly ignored me. I was one of many guests, and they were inured to the changing stream of people passing through their private, although outdoor, space.

I had booked my two-week stay at Jati Homestay through the internet. I was attracted by the reasonable price and scenic photographs of the adjacent rice field. Also, the patriarch of the family that ran the homestay was an artist. On my second day, I was invited by the artist's son, Dewa, to visit his father's studio. It was located on the second floor in one of the compound's buildings. The room was large and airy with generous windows overlooking the rice field. Immense canvasses leaned against the walls, and Dewa explained that they were waiting to be crated and shipped to a gallery in Germany for exhibition.

On my next visit to the studio, I met Jati, a slight man in his seventies. Most of his paintings were taller than he was. I introduced myself as a fellow artist, and I expressed admiration for the paintings that surrounded us. There were two major themes in the work he showed me. Some of the paintings had figures in bucolic scenes of daily Balinese life including women weaving baskets and presenting offerings. His second theme was that of exotic birds in jungle settings. Both series were painted in subtle pastel colors, and although quiet in tone, they were brimming with life and detail.

"What is the name of that beautiful bird?" I asked, gesturing towards a plump, soft grey bird in one of his paintings.

"Not real," he replied softly. "From here." He pointed to his head.

Struggling to express himself in English, he explained that all his work was painted not from real life but from his imagination. I was overwhelmed by the creativity and technical expertise of his work and expressed my admiration for his ability to paint so beautifully from his imagination alone. As I left his studio, I felt chastened by my own inability to create most of my art without reference material, whether actual objects, landscapes or photographs.

When my children were young, the subject matter of my art was domestic objects and still life scenes—an antique highchair, an overflowing toy box, an unmade bed or the remnants of a breakfast. As they grew, so did my range of subjects—flowers from our garden, the backyard and the front porch—things close to home. As time passed, my art depicted interiors of John's family cottage, fishing camps and landscapes glimpsed from our car on the long drive to the cottage. An etching from this time shows one of Andrew's toys—a G.I. Joe black plastic Cobra jet—sitting on a red checkered tablecloth. The plane looks as if it is sitting on a runway ready to fly out the window, which is in the background of the etching, towards trees and sky.

My art documented my family life, but it also became a way to deal with difficult periods in that life. The titles reflected those hard times—*Blue Flowers for a Blue Lady* and *Wildness Without, Chaos Within*. Making art was an escape, a way to use my hands and my head and something that provided pleasure and a sense of achievement. At a certain point, sexually suggestive shapes appeared in my flower images.

The spheres of influence for my art continued to broaden. Almost five years of extensive travel with a boyfriend produced landscapes of Alberta, Quebec, Newfoundland and Cyprus, where he lived.

Then my work took flight, both literally and figuratively. No longer earthbound, it dealt with images of infinite space. The work was inspired by photographs I took from airplane windows. Through them, I tried to communicate a sense of the ethereal nature of the sky thousands of feet above the earth with its vastness and mystery. It was my most intuitive and less naturalistic work.

Although there were potential subjects for my artwork at Jati Homestay, including the bubbling goldfish pond bordering the breakfast area, I didn't feel inspired to make art. Not only had I been humbled by the mastery of Jati's work, but I was also too stimulated by the noisy streets, high humidity and culture shock to settle down with the concentration needed to make art.

Rather than a single building, Gusti's Garden Bungalow consisted of multiple bungalows, and they were located, like Jati Homestay, at the back of the property, far from the street. There was a steep incline dotted by two-storey bungalows, most of which contained four suites. Generous porches had huge, cushioned bamboo chairs. The rooms were modest, like Jati's, but the garden was incredibly lush. Even better, down at the bottom of the many flights of stairs was a small swimming pool. For about five dollars a night more, I could stay at this wonderful place.

My only problem was that I felt guilty about not staying for the whole two weeks I'd booked at Jati Homestay. How could I break the news to Dewa or Butu, the two men I had been dealing with? I feared their retribution. It proved to be much easier than I expected, especially when I agreed to book a bicycle excursion and transport to my next destination through them. They were probably making a commission for arranging these trips, but I was happy to be able to move without feeling so guilty.

Making this decision gave my artist's block a nudge. I realized as I woke up on the morning of my move that the subject matter for my first piece of art created in Bali wasn't the beautiful landscape and flowers, not the ornate temples and shrines and not the people dressed in their colorful sarongs. It was the mosquito net hanging above my head and the patterning of the woven bamboo roof around it.

The mosquito net hung from the fourteen-foot-high ceiling, which was peaked in the middle. It hovered above me, white and gossamer. Seen from below, it looked like a huge trumpet flower with a flared, multi-scalloped edge. Dark wood ribs supported the basket weave bamboo on the ceiling. This seemingly mundane and simple subject appealed to me, probably because of the sensory overload I'd experienced since arriving in Bali. I had just enough time to make my first piece of art before leaving Jati Homestay.

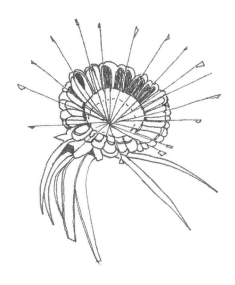

Chapter Twelve

I sat on the patterned stone steps that led, through an ornate portal, to the inner sanctum of Gusti's Garden Bungalow. The roosters seemed to have followed me here, and they still hadn't learned that they should crow only at sunrise.

I was transported here on the back of Butu's motorcycle, clutching his ample waist with my carry-on bag wedged between us. Maybe the case would act like an airbag in the collision I felt was inevitable. I couldn't decide whether to keep my eyes open or close them and not see the impact. I tried a combination of both. We survived the scary journey, and I waited for Butu to come back on his motorcycle with my large bag.

Gusti's was the next step up in the hierarchy of Balinese accommodation. The paths and alleyways were paved with stone mosaics, as opposed to Jati's uneven clay tiles, with muddy sections where the tiles had disappeared. The courtyards, open-sided temples and family buildings that I passed on the way to the bungalows were neat and tidy.

Every building had thresholds adorned with small offerings to the gods. The offerings, presented in small, square dishes woven from palm leaves, consisted of flowers, rice, spices, slices of banana, coins, sticks of incense, what appeared to be miniature Ritz crackers and even cigarettes. Everywhere I went in Ubud, these exquisite vessels adorned the doorsteps of shops, appeared at entrances to temples and at the foot of statues, sat on raised platforms in rice fields and dotted the rough, uneven clay tile of the sidewalks. I obviously needed protection afforded by the offering baskets from the malevolent sidewalk gods, who were forever trying to trip me up. More than once, I stumbled but caught myself before falling. It was the women's job to assemble the tiny offering baskets. I'd seen women making baskets in the inner courtyards of family compounds and shop girls making them while sitting on the steps of their stores.

At Gusti's, a simpler offering graced the tile floor of the porch of my bungalow. A small bit of banana leaf held some grains of cooked rice. I found out later that these were offerings made to evil spirits while the more elaborate miniature boxes were offerings made to the gods. Naively, I'd originally thought the rice-on-leaf objects were an ingenious form of ant trap.

I had much to learn about Balinese culture. Reading the Frommer's Guide to Bali and Lombok before leaving Canada helped. It emphasized the important role art played in the daily lives of the people. They didn't even have a word in their language for "artist" since, in one way or another, all of them were creative. They used many different forms of art—music, theatre, dance and the creation of paintings and sculpture—in the daily practice of their religion, a form of Hinduism called Hindu-Dharmaism.

My artist friends, Tony and Roswita, who had visited Bali, told me I would love the country for its natural beauty, the gentleness of its people and its culture.

"There's art everywhere," Tony said. "It's part of everyday life."

The people lived their lives as though they were part of an ongoing ceremony. Their art was part of that ceremony. Much time and effort was devoted to preparing offerings, temple decorations and food for ceremonies. There were very strict rules regarding entrance to temples. Special clothing had to be worn for specific ceremonies. Rather than try to understand and retain so much information at the beginning of my trip, I needed to learn slowly while immersing myself in the culture.

I was able to feel comfortable with Balinese value systems because of the importance art had played in my life.

"Lorna, with these marks, you should be a math teacher."

My grade twelve math teacher, Mr. Chase, placed the test paper on my desk. He'd circled the ninety-seven percent mark with a red pen. Yeah, I thought, and my dad wants me to be a lab technician. In his eyes that was an exceptional job that paid well.

There was no challenge for me in my math and science classes. If you studied hard enough and did the homework, it was easy to get almost perfect marks. Either right or wrong, there were no grey areas of interpretation in those subjects.

My art class: that was a different story. As much as I tried to do my best on all the projects, I never seemed to be able to get higher than eighty-two percent. It was a value judgment by my art teachers. The three of them, all men, based their marks not on how hard you'd worked on a project and the appearance of the end product but on such nebulous criteria as creativity and originality. Art class was where I was most challenged. Unlike other classes, where it was possible to earn an almost perfect mark by memorizing facts and figures, in art I had to learn to think up new ideas and express those ideas by making objects—drawings, paintings, photographs and sculpture.

"Dad," I said. "Teachers make good money. I'd like to be an art teacher."

We had reached a compromise. I could study Fine Art at university and then get my teaching degree.

Nearly all went according to plan. I was accepted into York Univer-

sity, married John between third and fourth years and enrolled in the Faculty of Education at the University of Toronto.

The plan derailed. The freedom of expression and self-motivated learning style I enjoyed in the Visual Arts program at York was totally different from the overly structured and punitive teaching program at the Faculty of Education. Two sessions of practice teaching confirmed for me that being a full-time art teacher in the public school system wasn't what I wanted to do. I realized that the time and energy commitments necessary to be a good teacher would leave no time or energy to continue making art. I could be a full-time teacher or an artist, not both. My decision disappointed both my father and my husband.

Nineteen years later, at the end of what I thought was a happy marriage and the birth of two children, John uttered his true sentiments.

"If I'd known you weren't going to be a teacher, I wouldn't have married you."

CHAPTER THIRTEEN

An eco/cultural bicycle tour provided an opportunity to learn more about Balinese life and culture. I was the last passenger picked up by the tour company's minivan. Joe, the Balinese guide, spoke English with a strange accent, the result of learning most of the language from his Australian boss. He was a friendly, attractive young man, genuinely eager to share his knowledge of the history and culture of his homeland. The group consisted of a beefy, red-faced couple in their forties from Australia, a couple of a similar age from Singapore, two couples in their thirties from Canada and a single woman close to my age, who described herself as a citizen of the world. Subsequently, I found out her name was Suzanne; she was a Brit by birth and had lived on the island of Corsica for twenty years. The Canadians were from Montreal, and although they were strangers, the men found common ground in the fortunes of the Habs (the Montreal Canadiens hockey team) and their recent trades.

A torrential downpour had just ended when Joe collected me from my porch. Overcast skies persisted on our one-hour drive up to Lake Batur, the largest lake in Bali, and the adjacent volcano. It was cool and windy as we exited the bus, but the wind wasn't strong enough to dissipate the fog that totally obscured the lake and the volcano. As we ate breakfast—my second of the day—in a restaurant on the lip of the volcano, the fog lifted long enough for a glimpse of the lake.

Back into the bus we piled, off to the pick-up point for the bicycles.

"Be sure to check your gears and brakes," Joe cautioned.

We set out down a small rural lane as the sun struggled to shine through the overcast sky. The tour company designed the route to be mostly on obscure country lanes so we avoided the madness of the main roads. Although I was intimidated at first, driving on the left side of the road became second nature.

The pain in my fingers from squeezing the brakes confirmed that this was, as promised, a downhill drive. We coasted past open stretches of rice fields and through leafy, shaded tunnels of vegetation and tiny rural villages. In the villages, children ran to the side of the lanes, hands held aloft as a signal for a "high five." Some yelled out in English, "Where are you from?" as we zipped past their family compounds. Mostly, we were welcomed by smiles. Only once did I feel like an unwanted foreign intruder when a boy of about ten spat in my direction as we passed a group of school children. His action made me question whether this form of eco-tourism was a mutually beneficial exchange between two cultures. Here we were, the rich (at least compared to them), white interlopers gaping at his culture and way of life. Did he feel resentful for this intrusion? Was I trying to read too much into his rude gesture? Maybe he was just acting macho to impress his friends.

Our first of many stops was to have a "Kodak Moment," or, as Joe joked, a "Canon Moment" at a spot where terraced rice fields ascended a steep hill. Joe explained the elaborate irrigation system and how the farmers worked together to ensure that all levels were irrigated. The farmer owning the lowest field was in charge of the water supply because he had the most to lose if the water didn't reach his field through mismanagement of the resources.

Our next stop was at a fruit and coffee farm located on the side of a hill, an establishment that was obviously staged as a tourist destination. Joe identified various plants and trees, explained how cinnamon was harvested from the bark of the tree, what the ginseng plant looked like and how the pods of the cocoa tree were used.

We saw coffee beans roasted over an open fire. We sat down in a lovely hillside pavilion, and a young woman wearing a sarong presented us with six complimentary cups of various types of tea, cocoa and coffee. The specialty of this particular coffee plantation was Luwak coffee. This coffee had become famous in the West because of the movie "The Bucket List." Jack Nicholson's character brags about being able to buy the most expensive coffee in the world. Coffee beans are eaten by civet cats, one of which we saw cowering in a cage. The beans are fermented in the journey through the cat's digestive system and are excreted whole in their poop. Apparently, the civets are picky, choosing to eat only the most delectable and best coffee beans. We were offered, for the nominal price of about three dollars, a sample of this rare coffee, which would have been sold for forty dollars a cup in more affluent countries. Those of us who were brave enough to sample the coffee received a small green ceramic pot.

"Let coffee powder settle to bottom of cup," our hostess said. "Better without sugar or milk."

It didn't taste like cat poop (not that I've ever sampled cat poop), and the flavor was smooth and mild. The only unpleasant characteristic was the muddy sludge left in the bottom of the cup.

Next, we were given samples of various types of local fruit. The passion fruit was sweet and seedy. One fruit had the taste and texture of lychee, and the honey mango, although green on the outside, did taste like honey. The snakefruit looked like its namesake—reddish-brown scaly skin—and was rather dry and tasted like a Delicious apple.

"Snakefruit good for Bali belly," Joe said.

Suzanne, having passed on the other fruit samples, said, "I'll try this one." Perhaps her digestive tract wasn't in synch with the rigors of being a world traveler, and she needed its medicinal benefits.

Our third stop was a revelation. A rural family, for monetary compensation, gave the eco-touring company permission for its customers to view their family compound.

The first structure in the compound was the grandmother's—a woman whose age was apparently unknown. She lived there with the families of her sons, her daughters having moved out, when they married, to the compounds of their husbands. We entered her kitchen, which was a tiny, soot-covered, dark and dirty space with an earth floor. There was a fire pit and a few battered pans. There was no refrigerator, no sink, no cupboards; none of the utensils and appliances that we consider essential in our kitchens. She squatted on her small roofed porch weaving bamboo strips.

"She's so old, she's not expected to work," Joe said, "but she likes to keep busy."

She smiled graciously at us and seemed to enjoy having her picture taken.

Each son's family had its own kitchen in the compound, but family members didn't normally eat together. Food was prepared early in the day; each person helped themselves when they were hungry.

The compound was laid out like the human body. The family temple, or head, was first in line. Then platforms where offerings were prepared represented the heart. Next were the kitchens and sleeping buildings—the stomach—and, finally, the toilets and animal pens— the legs. Legs are considered unclean, which is why sarongs are used to cover them during ceremonies and to enter temples. There were two cows and a bunch of pigs in small concrete holding pens with the toilets off to one side. One of our group chose to utilize a nearby tree rather than use the "facilities."

We walked back up the side of the compound where the family business was located. This family wove bamboo mats, and women sat on the ground weaving long strips of bamboo. A little boy, less than three years old, had a knife in his hand "helping" his mother with her work.

Further along,, men were engaged in their work, "stroking their cocks," Joe joked. The men of the family ran afternoon cockfights for the other village men, and they stroked their fighting birds in preparation. Cockfighting is legal only in certain ceremonial functions related to the temples. These enterprising men were capitalizing on the human compulsion to gamble, and the police rarely interfered.

"Looks to me," Suzanne said, "like the women do all the work and the men have all the fun."

Indeed, the men socialized, with cigarette in hand or mouth; the women wove. This view of rural Bali gave me a new appreciation for the privileges of my lifestyle.

We stopped twice in the rice fields. The first time we got off our bikes, we walked precariously, in single file, along the narrow, raised, packed earth that bordered each section of the field. We ducked under lines adorned with all sorts of colorful scraps. Tattered plastic bags alternated with bits of shiny metal cut from empty soft drink cans. Pieces of worn-out clothing fluttered in the breeze. The rice in these particular fields was almost ripe, and these colorful bits tied to string functioned as scarecrows. As added insurance, women were stationed in little raised, covered bamboo stands among the fields. They were paid by the owners of the fields they guarded with some of the harvested rice so it was in their interests to make certain as little of the crop as possible went to marauding birds. To help pass the time, they were weaving the baskets that were used in the temple ceremonies.

The second rice field stop was at a place where the rice was ripe. Some of the workers, who this time included both men and women, wielded curved long-handled knives to cut the sheaves. Others carried these bundles on their backs to a spot where plastic tarps had been laid out on the ground. Three women banged the rice sheaves against a rough board, about four feet by four feet, propped up at a forty-five degree angle. The rice husks flew onto the adjacent tarps. The sheaves were passed to another woman, who separated the dried-out parts from the green parts. They put the dried-out parts back on the fields as mulch and fed the green stems to the cows. Duck flocks, herded onto the harvested fields, scavenged the rice husks that had dropped on the fields. The farmers used all of the rice plant; nothing was wasted.

We witnessed the next step in the processing of the rice as we rode through the villages. The rice pods needed to be dried in the sun before they were fed into machines that removed the husks. The drying was sometimes done in courtyards, but it was also done on tarps laid out on the roads in the villages. Our guide rode right through the rice, and the rest of us respectfully guided our bikes around the tarps.

We passed through many villages. Our route was a maze of country roads and village lanes, and at one point, even our guide, Joe, became lost in the confusion of turns and had to ask for directions. Another time, we lost Suzanne. Joe rode back and found her blithely taking photographs of a village temple. I guess she reasoned that since Bali was a small island she couldn't stay lost for long.

Riding our bicycles along a muddy trail beside one field, we came across a woman sitting in the narrow irrigation stream taking a bath. At a larger river, a mother bathed her rather plump son. It was rare to see any overweight people in Bali. At a different spot in the same river, women washed their clothes.

After a fifteen mile ride, all of us passed up the opportunity to ride for an additional forty-five minutes uphill to where we were to have lunch. Some of the younger members of our group, who had said they were avid cyclists back home, reneged on the vow they made earlier to complete the uphill portion of the tour.

Comparing notes with my fellow cyclists about our Balinese shopping experiences, I learned that bargaining was expected. They were surprised that I'd paid full price for my sarong and bragged about their five dollar sarong purchases. My natural aversion to shopping and bargaining guaranteed that I purchased very little in that first week.

July 1991.

Feeling sad and insecure, I came out of the bathroom into our elegant room at the Chateau Frontenac Hotel in Quebec City.

"You look like a giant strawberry," John said, glancing up briefly.

He was reading what he hoped would be his acceptance speech as the newly-elected president of his profession's national institute. We had driven here, to the city where I was born, without our children. Staying at the Chateau Frontenac, a grand hotel that looked like a castle, was supposed to be a treat for me to celebrate my fortieth birthday. It also co-incided with the annual convention that my husband was here to attend.

The garishly patterned dress, with its oversize red and black flowers on a white background, swamped my skeletal body. I'd lost twenty pounds because of the stress and anxiety from what was happening in my relationship with my husband. The only foods my stomach and bowels could tolerate were oatmeal, mashed potatoes and applesauce.

"I thought it would look better when I bought it," he said. "I paid a lot of money for it. It came from the MB Boutique." He named a well-known Canadian designer.

The huge shoulder pads, a common feature in the clothing of that time, made me look like a middle linebacker. I'd pinned together the sides of the overlapping, v-necked blouse so as to camouflage my scrawny neck and lack of cleavage. I'd also pinned the waistband of the skirt so it would stay up. The voluminous, gathered skirt hung almost to the floor, making me look like a pitiful waif trying on someone else's clothes.

For the previous few years, I regularly received a dress purchased by John as either a birthday or Christmas gift, so I could better look the part of the wife of a successful city planner. I hated to shop, especially for clothes. My taste in dressy clothing leaned toward a slightly eclectic mix of treasures from the Sally Ann and vintage dresses that were hand-me-downs from John's mother. My everyday wardrobe consisted of comfortable, baggy jeans and my husband's old plaid wool shirts. The shirts were practical on two accounts—they kept me warm as I worked on my art in my damp basement studio and they were baggy enough to disguise the fact that I seldom wore a bra.

It didn't seem to matter what I wore at home anyway. I was usually in bed by the time John got home from his meetings at work. When he *was home, he was distracted, cold and not at all interested in what was happening. The only exception to this indifference was his interest in our son's hockey games.*

On the advice of "people at work," he had upgraded his own wardrobe. I was forbidden from opening our credit card bill, which, up to that point in our marriage, I'd always paid, along with all the household bills. His work—and a certain person there—became the most important thing in his life. My special birthday dress was hideous; so was our marriage. Years later, it occurred to me that my dress might have been selected by his girlfriend, just like his new expensive suits and overcoat. He looked good; I looked bad.

CHAPTER FOURTEEN

Sitting beside Suzanne in the minibus, we exchanged information about our respective travel plans. She planned to move the following day to a retreat for an intensive session of yoga, meditation and healthy food.

"Would you like to join me?" she asked. "It's supposed to be one of the best holistic retreats in Bali."

"Sorry," I said, "It sounds great, but I've arranged to go to Amed." I had my doubts that her constant chatter would be held in check by the enforced serenity of the meditation retreat.

My second offer of the day to join fellow travelers came as I sought the cool refuge of the pool at Gusti's Garden Bungalow. Two young women joined me, and because the pool was so small, we were soon chatting. They were from the States and had been traveling in Southeast Asia for several months. They told me of their amazing experiences kayaking on a river in Borneo. I found out that one of them was also an artist. Bobbing in the azure pool, we established a convivial bond.

"We've found a bungalow on the edge of a rice field nearby. It's got a kitchen where we can cook our own meals and save some money. We're moving there tomorrow."

"Sounds good," I said. I didn't want to dampen their enthusiasm about their new home by pointing out the connection between rice fields, mosquitoes and nocturnal serenading amphibians and insects, not to mention rats.

"Would you like to share it with us? There's an extra bed."

I suspected from details of their story and the way their bodies brushed up against each other in the small pool that their relationship was more than that of traveling companions and that I was being asked to join a possible ménage à trois.

"That's very generous of you, but I've made plans to move on to Amed. I'm really looking forward to snorkeling there," I said. I was flattered by their offer but didn't think I was ready for a same sex relationship with not one, but two partners.

"Mom, you should give it a try. You've had such bad luck with men," my daughter Alison said.

We had just found out that the young woman Andrew was dating had attended the wedding of her mother to another woman. Same-sex marriages had recently become legal in Ontario.

Alison continued her sales pitch on the merits of female partners.

"Women understand each other. They're in tune with each other's feelings, unlike some of the men you've dated." She had disliked most of the men I'd been involved with, believing that they had not treated me well.

"This is a strange conversation," I said. "Imagine a daughter encouraging her mother to try a lesbian relationship. Women are great as friends, but they lack the physical attributes of a male."

Alison rolled her eyes. "Too much information," she said.

I'd prearranged my transfer from Ubud to Amed with Dewa at

Jati Homestay. Butu, who was to be my driver, showed up at Gusti's Garden Bungalow a day early. Exhausted by the bicycle tour the previous day, I was still in bed when he came knocking on my door just before nine in the morning. I scrambled to find a t-shirt, having slept only in my panties.

"You not ready?" Butu said when he saw my undressed state.

"Butu, Dewa and I arranged the drive to Amed for tomorrow, not today," I replied.

"But have car today," he insisted.

"No, that's not right, I wrote the day in my book." I grabbed my notebook from the bedside table. "Look, my memory's so bad I wrote down the date in two places."

Butu looked at the page, shrugged, capitulated and left.

Not surprisingly, a different man knocked on my door the next morning. Nyoman was a quiet man in his late thirties. I confirmed with him that we would stop at some of the tourist attractions en route to Amed. He loaded my bags into the vehicle he was driving. I was glad it wasn't a motorcycle but a minivan. I headed to the passenger's seat on the right side of the vehicle. He looked puzzled at my choice of seat, and I remembered that the driver's wheel was on the right.

As agreed, we stopped at the Elephant Temple, the Bat Cave Temple and a historically important town called Klungkung. Although he didn't accompany me into the temples, Nyoman graciously tied my sarong and sash in the Balinese style at each stop. Although my sarong was authentically (and expensively) Balinese, my sash, which I'd brought with me from Canada, was a scarf adorned with cats. I hoped it wasn't inappropriate for temples, and I was relieved when nobody seemed to take offense at its subject matter.

Self-appointed guides tried to offer their services at each temple. At our first stop, the Elephant Temple, I hired one of these guides as he seemed determined to be at my side anyway. I discovered his English skills were not up to the challenge of providing information that I could understand.

Our next stop was *Pura Goa Lawah*, or Bat Cave Temple, one of the nine directional temples in Bali that protect the island from evil spirits. *Pura Goa Lawah*, the sacred site for Brahma, the Hindu god of creation, was also a popular site for the deification of a deceased family member's soul. For me, this spooky cave—its walls vibrating with the squirming of thousands of bats—wasn't an uplifting pilgrimage destination. The Balinese, however, believed that every living organism has both good and evil spirits. Perhaps the pilgrims, who sought the highest incarnation for the souls of departed family members, thought that their grief could be banished to a symbolic dark cave while their loved ones' souls soared into reincarnation as happier, nobler beings.

At first, I didn't see the bats, but as my eyes adjusted to the dim light at the mouth of the cave, I became aware of their movement, as if the walls of the cave were breathing like some huge dark creature. I was transported back to a time in my life when my mind was a gloomy cave teeming with ugly thoughts and where I physically retreated to my darkened bedroom.

February 14, 1992

Maybe writing will air my feelings without boring people with the same thing over and over. Feeling really depressed—all the ads about Valentine's Day are like a bad joke. Need to have the courage and strength to say to John that it's all over and to stop screwing me up with this idea of a "temporary" separation. God, give me the strength to get on with it. God, give me a reason to keep on with everything. Show me the right thing to do. Make the hurt go away. I still get an awful sinking feeling in my gut when I think of him with that other woman. Maybe I'll just hibernate for the rest of the winter.

March 4, 1992

Couldn't get to sleep last night. Felt a little spaced out from the medication. Seemed to have trouble focusing my eyes. John apparently saw me from a street car at Queen and Roncesvalles. He's in a mellow mood again and asked to talk to me. Had feelings of emptiness, despair and disbelief again like a void in my stomach. Can't believe the person I met and loved for so long can change into such a different person. I thought our love was so intense, it would last forever. Keep thinking of our courting days and when we first met. There is an unreality to my life—things are just not right.

Ash Wednesday at the church. Ashes of penitence on my forehead. In his sermon, Merv suggested that God's infinite and ultimate purpose for us should transcend the here and now. Ashes of penitence, forgiveness.

September 26, 1992

Bad, bad night—booze and pills. Couldn't reach anyone. Bed at 3 am. Totally knocked out.

March 4, 1993

Shitty day, shitty mood, shitty life.

What a strange connection my mind had made between a slightly sinister and creepy bat cave and my black thoughts and obsessive behavior when my marriage died. My own reincarnation into a happier, nobler being had taken years.

CHAPTER FIFTEEN

Nyoman, my driver, described a local dish made from breadfruit, pineapple and other interesting ingredients. I asked him to stop for lunch at a place where we could sample it. Instead, he deposited me on the doorstep of a restaurant high in the mountains. It was obviously a tourist restaurant, where I was subjected to an overpriced, insipid buffet. Although the food wasn't very good, I didn't mind so much because Nyoman was probably eating free behind the scenes. The panoramic view across and down into the terraced rice fields was worth putting up with lukewarm, bland food.

He was happy to stop at a place I'd specifically requested. Possibly, he would receive a commission if I bought anything there. It was a textile workshop in Sideman, identified in my guidebook as one of Bali's weaving villages. Its specialty was a type of woven textile called *songket*, which incorporated gold and silver threads. When I asked to see the workshop, the middle-aged male owner directed me down a long flight of stairs to a shed. The dim and dusty room had a few bare light bulbs hanging from cords and not many windows. About twenty-five of the approximately forty wooden looms sat idle. At the others, women threw shuttles back and forth and pounded foot pedals. The noise, as the shuttles clacked and the pedals thudded, overwhelmed me. I could only imagine how deafening it would be if all the looms were in operation. I noticed one young woman who was particularly quick. She appeared to be only a child.

None of the women were weaving *songket* fabric, but all of their work was complex and wonderfully patterned. Some of them were weaving *ikat* fabric, where the pattern is revealed as the variably-dyed weft threads interact with the warp threads to produce a kind of zig-zag or pixilated design.

I climbed the stairs to the shop. Tables were heaped with lengths of fabric, but I couldn't see any price tags.

"How much is this?" I asked the owner. I showed him a piece of dark blue fabric embellished with lines of gold thread.

"That *songet* cloth. Very special." The price he quoted was much higher than I expected. No wonder my driver was willing to stop at this shop. My budget wouldn't allow such an expensive purchase.

I picked up a small table runner from a different table. It had red and orange stripes and was woven from thick cotton threads.

"And this?" I said, holding up the simple piece of fabric.

"One hundred thousand rupiah," he replied.

I could afford this price—about ten dollars. He seemed disappointed at my selection.

I hoped that in a small way my purchase was supporting the work of the women in the unsophisticated, dark workshop below.

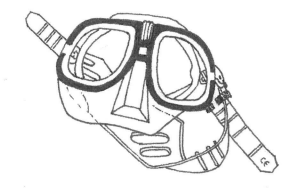

Chapter Sixteen

Dewa, from Jati Homestay, had recommended a place to stay in Amed called Double One Villas. Taking in its breathtaking location in a garden overlooking the sea, I thought I'd moved closer to the inner sanctum of heaven. My first room at Double One Villas, one of three rooms located underneath the reception area, was huge and beautiful, but it proved to be too close to the road. The sound of motorbikes, headed to the market at the nearest large village, started early in the morning. I am not a morning person. I moved down the hill closer to the water to escape the noise. There, I had my own one-room cottage, what the Balinese called a villa. For about five dollars extra a night, this room had a mini refrigerator, a nicer bathroom and air conditioning, if I wanted to use it. The sound of the waves was louder here but not as loud as at the two expensive oceanfront villas where the water noises would have had me peeing all night. The price per day for this upgraded room, including breakfast and a bottle of water, was equivalent to about thirty-two dollars.

"Is there a discount for staying longer than one night?" I asked the man showing me the room.

"No," he said.

"Then how about an extra bottle of water each day?"

He nodded, and I felt good about my newly acquired bargaining skills.

After breakfast and my move to the new room, I went snorkeling—almost in front of the hotel. The water was wavy so it was murky near the shore, but once I was far enough out, it cleared. I began to see many wonderful fish but was disappointed by the condition of the coral. I floated and bobbed in the waves for an hour.

As I was coming out of the water a man, who appeared to be in his early twenties, approached me.

"Lady, not good snorkel here," he said. "Too rough. No coral. No fish."

"But I saw many nice fish," I replied.

"I take you better place. Many fish. Big coral. Special place with shipwreck." He pointed further along the shore.

"Maybe tomorrow," I said as I bent to take off my flippers.

I finished off the morning with a swim in the pool located beside the beach. It was a bit small for swimming lengths, but was fine for my improvised water aerobics. As I exercised, I watched an exquisitely colored bird, the same size as a hummingbird, flitting from flower to flower on a bush nearby.

This was only my first day at Double One Villas in Amed Beach, and it was so peaceful and scenic that I considered staying a long time. I'd seen only two other guests, so the place was quiet—ideal for personal introspection. The pouring rain that afternoon provided a good excuse to postpone the introspection and take a nap.

CHAPTER SEVENTEEN

The rats must have hitched a ride from Ubud to Amed. During the night, I was woken up by the scratching sound of some creature, either at one of the low front windows, or in the woven bamboo ceiling. I'd discovered none of the distinctive calling cards left by the rodents in the dresser drawer at Jati Homestay. Once totally awake, I noticed flashes of lightning from the direction of the ocean. The panoramic lighting effects were soon accompanied by the booming sound of thunder and then by the drumming of a torrential deluge of rain. These storms were a daily and/or nightly occurrence since Bali was still in the November to March rainy season. Unlike most tropical storms, this one lasted all night. Fortunately, the drumming of the rain and the pounding of the waves covered up the annoying scratching sounds.

It was still overcast the next morning. As I ate breakfast in the open-air dining area by the sea, I was joined by the young man who the previous day had tried to sell me his services as a snorkeling guide. I thought he wouldn't show up because the water was murky from the night's storm. It was the low season for tourism, and looking for a source of income, he insisted that snorkeling in the protected cove would be fine.

His "transport" to the snorkeling site was parked beside the reception area near the road. It was a black Honda motorbike. As before, with my transport between accommodations in Ubud by Butu, there was no sign of helmets. I'd come to Bali for adventure so I climbed on behind him. As I clamped my hands around his waist I asked him his name.

"John," he said.

I was risking my life on a motorcycle driven by a man who had the same name as my ex-husband. Not surprisingly, I had some trust issues with him. Twenty years ago it was a different season, a different country and a different man, but their names were the same.

October 1991

The late autumn light, with its particular clarity and low angle, flooded the breakfast room through the bay window. Enough of the leaves had fallen from the sugar maple tree just outside the window to allow the light to penetrate into the room. I sat facing the window, blinking in the strong light and not really seeing my husband's features as his back was to the light. He sat in one of the mismatched wooden chairs I'd rescued from the curb in front of a neighbor's house.

A whiff of solvent floated up from my basement studio where I'd earlier cleaned up ink after proofing a new etching. The image on that plate was of our unmade bed in the master bedroom directly above our heads. The tangle of striped sheets and floral patterned bedspread mirrored the random jumble of almost naked branches seen in the background through the bay window. Many months later, the title of that etching would reflect what was happening in my life at the time: "Wildness Without, Chaos Within."

I was aware of the dark shape of my husband's body silhouetted in the window, but his face was blurred by my tears.

"Get a real job, like normal people." The hateful words stung me. "Our kids don't need you to be home, and your art adds nothing to our income."

In one fell swoop, he had obliterated my self-esteem by denigrating my most important roles, a mother to two children, aged eleven and fourteen, and an artist. The income I made from part-time stints teaching children's art and as an arts administrator had been enough to pay only for studio rental fees and childcare costs when the children were younger. Then, I bought a used etching press and set up a crude studio in our cramped, dark basement when the children were older so I could be there for them when they came home from school. I earned a bit of extra income each day after school by babysitting a child who was a close friend of my daughter and by being a cleaning lady at my parents' apartment once a week. It wasn't enough money to contribute to the lifestyle my husband wanted.

Two months later, December's meager light didn't penetrate to the kitchen next to the breakfast nook. The overhead globular light fixture caused an unflattering gleam on my husband's forehead. This time he wasn't sitting on a chair; he delivered the words of betrayal standing up, as though ready to flee.

"You and I have nothing in common except the children. She works with me and understands what I do," he said.

"I love her."

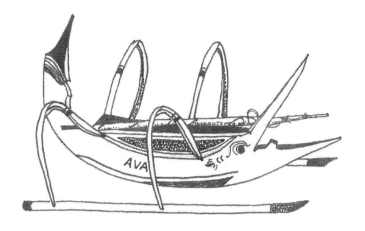

Chapter Eighteen

The road was slick from the night's rain. Passing through one village, I had to lift up my feet as we splashed through a huge pond caused by the overflow of a river. Since the road hugged the hilly coast, it was convoluted, up steep inclines and down through hollows and around turns that doubled back on themselves. Although this drive didn't have the same dangers as the one in the motorcycle-and-car-clogged streets of Ubud, it had its own white-knuckle, eye-closing challenges. At one point, a skinny white dog meandered off the road just in time for us to miss him and roar past.

Twenty scary minutes later, we arrived at our destination and climbed down steps to a beach. It was picturesque with many *jukung* pulled up on the rocky shore. These long, skinny boats, built from single tree trunks, had outrigger extensions on both sides. They were fishing boats and occasionally transported tourists to coves like this one. The outriggers were made from hollow bamboo logs. All had colorful, furled sails, but most also had a small outboard motor. We ducked under the outriggers and sat down to don our snorkeling equipment. Now I had to trust this young man as a snorkeling guide as well as a driver.

"Your real name isn't John, is it?" I was hoping that he'd used it only because it was easy for tourists to remember.

He hesitated before answering. "I'm Suki."

Since Suki didn't have snorkeling fins, I easily kept up with him in the water. As he guaranteed, the water was calmer and clearer here. The coral wasn't damaged by heavy wave action like in front of the hotel. The overcast sky slightly muted the color intensity of the fish and coral. At this depth—ten to fifteen feet—most of the coral was huge. The fissured surface was like the brains of giants. Filigreed, lacy fan coral shimmered in the current.

Tiny, electric-blue fish played tag in their underwater garden. Fish nipping at hard corals produced a sort of grinding noise. Four-inch-long, yellow and black angelfish glided by gracefully. Curious ser-geant major fish, with their iridescent blue, yellow and black stripes, ventured closer to check out these alien invaders of their kingdom. I must have looked as exotic to them as they did to me because of my white bathing suit covered with a pattern of multi-hued tropical flowers. The sight of me in the strange looking mask, a snorkel grow-ing from my head, the elongated fins at the end of my legs, must have been as good a source of entertainment for the fish as the fish were for me.

Snorkeling was one of the reasons I came to Bali. It had become a passion since my first snorkeling experience on a trip to Cuba, six-teen years earlier. The sensation of escaping to another world, where beauty and adventure beckoned, was addictive. When seeking new travel destinations, whether it was with a succession of boyfriends or on cruises with my mother, those that offered the prospect of good snorkeling were hard to resist. This passion, ignited in Cuba and nourished by trips to Roatan, Cozumel, St. Martin and Curacao, finally led me to Bali.

Three of my serious relationships since my marriage ended were with men who not only shared my interest in snorkeling but also had the same first name, Bob. Even more unusual, all were Virgos whose birthdays were within two weeks of each other in September. My daughter liked to point out that the coincidences ended there since they had been born in three different decades.

On cruises with my mom, I sampled the snorkeling delights of Tahiti, Bora Bora, Moorea, Huahine, Hawaii, the Great Barrier Reef and Antigua. A four-and-a-half year relationship with a Brit living in Cyprus—Bob number two—resulted in snorkeling adventures in Belize, the Red Sea and Gan, the most southerly island in the Maldives. Gan's isolated location in the Indian Ocean meant that few tourists ventured there. The coral was pristine, undamaged by overuse through diving, snorkeling and fishing. In Bali, I could wade into the water from the beach anytime I wanted and snorkel for as long as I wanted by myself.

Snorkeling with a partner is a unique way to test one's compatibility with that person and make an assessment about their character. The most satisfying dynamic was swimming side by side pointing out discoveries of unique fish or spectacles on the ocean floor that the other person might have missed. Neither person dominated in choice of direction or speed. Both could see if the other person needed to stop and adjust their mask or whether they were just lingering over an especially beautiful spot.

A second style of snorkeling was one partner leading the way with—ideally—the other person following close behind. Sometimes, though, the follower stopped to look closer at a fish or some coral or simply to adjust equipment and soon the leader was far ahead, oblivious to having lost his partner. The follower had to abandon her leisurely contemplation of the underwater sights in order to catch up.

The worst kind of snorkeling partner was the one who immediately took off on a mission to cover as much water in as short a time as possible. I had the misfortune to be abandoned by my partner—Bob number one—as I was thrown by a crashing wave onto a coral reef and pulled under by the fast current. He seemed surprised, when he returned to the boat that had brought us out to the reef, that I was both scared and angry. The scar on my leg from a coral scrape is a souvenir of that relationship.

I knew that my most recent relationship—not a Bob—was in jeopardy on our first trip together when he refused to join me in the water on our second snorkeling excursion. On our first outing, despite having represented himself as an experienced snorkeler and former dive master, he had trouble with both his mask and snorkel. The next time we went, he stayed on the shore while I snorkeled alone. Even worse, he didn't warn me when he saw the red flag hoisted on shore—the signal for dangerous water conditions. He could have come to help me get out of the water safely but didn't, and the waves bashed me against the concrete steps leading out of the water. Another scar, both literally and figuratively, added to the relationship score card.

December 2010

It was nine-thirty on a Thursday night on the small Caribbean island. I'd just stepped out into the humid air on the balcony overlooking the swimming pool. It was an infinity pool so the dark turquoise water seemed to extend into the shimmering ocean. There was a distant glimmer of lights from the huge resorts on the neighbouring island.

I needed to escape from the room with its marble floor, cushioned wicker chairs and the huge in-room Jacuzzi because of the snoring, naked man sprawled out in the middle of the king-size bed. I'd just managed to remove the heavy ornamental bedspread that was captured under one of his legs. The points of that starfish-shaped body—arms, legs and head— were flung to the edges of the bed, leaving little room for me.

It was too early for me to try to get to sleep even if I could ignore the grunting snoring sounds. How had I found myself in this posh resort on an idyllic island, with a man I hardly knew passed out on the bed?

I could blame it on the unreal expectations of internet dating. Shared interests in traveling and snorkeling had catapulted a fledgling relationship into a travel adventure within a month and a half of making contact through an online dating site.

The first phone call, with its exchange of information—not unlike a job interview—was promising. He didn't have the same first name as three of my former boyfriends. Maybe that wasn't a positive thing. At the age of fifty-nine, my memory for names was failing. The same name would have prevented mistakes, particularly in a moment of passion. That problem proved to be irrelevant. He was hard of hearing and would likely not be wearing his hearing aids during intimate encounters.

His marital situation was similar to mine, a divorce long ago and multiple relationships since. Family was as important to him as it was to me. He had four adult children and one grandchild. What had attracted me to his profile on the dating website was the charming photograph of him reading to his grandson. I had two adult children and two grandchildren. He, like me, was the primary chauffeur for his elderly mother. He had even traveled recently with her to Honduras, and I likewise enjoyed cruises and trips with my mother.

He liked dancing and we had similar tastes in music. He liked dark chocolate, scotch and red wine. He, like me, had played hockey, although he had not kept it up. I was still playing once a week in a "girls" hockey league. I love being on, near or in the water, and I particularly love snorkeling in tropical waters. One of his jobs had involved ship navigation and diving. We both loved to travel, and since we were self-employed, we had the necessary time and resources. He stayed fit by working out at the gym, primarily by riding a stationary bike. I prefer a moving one that provides a changing view of the lakefront near my home. This difference in cycling styles didn't appear to be a deal breaker due to all our other shared interests.

"Sounds like we have lots in common," he said. "How about meeting to test out the chemistry?"

This was a dating site code word, which basically meant, "Do you look anything at all like your photograph?" It was commonly acknowledged that most women posted a flattering photograph that was possibly up to ten years old. Men tended to enhance their profiles by saying they had an athletic body, and they were at least five feet nine inches tall.

My potential new mate surprised me by suggesting a meeting place different from the usual Starbucks, Second Cup or Tim Horton's coffee shops. These businesses must be very happy with online dating sites as a way to boost their bottom line. He proposed meeting on the next Sunday afternoon at a club/bar/restaurant that was conveniently located for both of us. This was a promising sign.

"We can have a drink and listen to one of my favourite bands. They play golden oldies from the sixties to eighties—great dancing music," he said.

This wasn't going to be one of those standard coffee dates.

At the agreed upon date and time, I pulled into a parking spot at the place where we were to meet. I glanced to my left and noticed a man sitting in a car in the next space. During our telephone conversation, I'd asked how I would recognize him, half-joking that he might not look like his online photo. The man in the car next to me was wearing a navy blue jacket and light blue golf shirt just like those described by my date.

I smiled tentatively. He smiled back. He did look like his photograph. As we stepped out of our cars and greeted each other, I realized he had stretched the truth regarding his height. With my flat shoes, our eyes were on the same level. I'd always thought myself to be five feet five-and-a-half inches tall but was shocked to discover at my recent physical that I'd shrunk to five feet four inches. I considered being more flexible on my height expectations if the other personal data in his profile was closer to the mark.

We settled into a booth and exchanged pleasantries across the table. I ordered a glass of red wine and was surprised when he ordered a soft drink. Perhaps he doesn't need the benefit of alcohol to be personable and witty, I thought. As the music started, he slipped onto the bench beside me to get a better sightline to the band and to make it easier to hear each other above the loud music. He had lost one of his hearing aids, so we had to communicate by yelling into each other's "good" ear. Hearing loss proved to be one of the challenges of middle-age dating.

I felt comfortable with him, so I didn't mind when he took my hand. The rock-and-roll music was loud and enticing, and soon we were on the dance floor, jiving to the music like familiar dance partners. True to his profile, he really did like to dance and was very confident and proficient. My pleasure showed: a cheek-to-cheek grin never left my face as we swung and twirled to the music. Dancing led to dinner, with a second glass of wine for me and more soft drinks for him.

It felt natural to part at the end of the evening with a sweet kiss. With a smile on my face, I drove home, sat down at my computer and removed my profile from the dating website. Why keep looking when my dream match seemed to have arrived in my inbox?

Things progressed quickly. He was a good cook who enjoyed preparing dinner for me. He was proud of his wine-making abilities, and we consumed several bottles as we prepared and ate dinner. I learned of his fondness for single malt scotch and brought him a bottle as a thank-you gift for all the fine dinners he'd prepared. We watched movies and hockey games at his place and enjoyed an afternoon swim together in his condo's pool.

Within a month and a half, we were planning a trip together. He owned a membership similar to a timeshare at a chain of resorts in the Caribbean. My share of the trip's cost was affordable. Knowing my passion for snorkeling, he booked a resort with a shallow coral reef just offshore.

The resort was beautiful. Its relatively small size guaranteed personal attention from the staff. We were given a welcoming martini as we registered, and I was presented with a fragrant red carnation. Each time we settled in comfortable chairs in the lobby bar or sat down on chaises near the pool, we were offered our choice of drinks. These included not only the rum drinks offered by the standard all-inclusive Caribbean resorts but also martinis and margaritas. There was a martini menu with brand name spirits and liqueurs. The margaritas were made with fresh lime juice so they didn't have the lurid green color and artificial syrup taste of inferior margaritas at less opulent resorts.

I thought little of it as my companion started off each morning with several mimosas made with freshly squeezed oranges and sparkling wine. Several glasses of white wine at lunch were followed by scotch-on-the-rocks in the afternoon, at least two bottles of red wine with dinner and several generous snifters of brandy in the evening. Without asking, he ordered wine at lunch for me, but after a couple of days, I begged off, protesting that it made me too sleepy in the afternoon.

We enjoyed socializing with several younger couples in the evening. On the second evening, my companion's voice became louder with each brandy and his words slurred. Abruptly, he said it was time to go. By the time I came out of the bathroom, he had passed out on the bed. The next evening, he wavered his way to the elevator, put the pass card the wrong way in the door lock and was already prone on the bed before I'd even made it to the bathroom.

I was still awake about an hour later when I felt him moving and then heard his bare feet on the marble floor. The next thing I heard was a loud crash. I pounded the light switch beside the bed and discovered an upsetting sight. Our large room was on two levels. The bed was on the top level with a large Jacuzzi bath tub flush to that floor. The sitting area was two steps down. In the dark, he had turned left at the foot of the bed instead of turning right for the bathroom and had fallen down the steps. Luckily, he had missed falling into the Jacuzzi. Also lucky for him, his fall had been partially broken by a wicker arm chair. I rushed to his side, looked for blood, found none, and then asked if he was okay. He didn't appear to have any limbs at weird angles. I helped him to his feet, and he proceeded on his unusual path to the bathroom, returned and climbed into bed without a word.

Strangely, he said nothing the next day about his previous night's misadventure. Later that day, he complained about having a sore back and couldn't think of a reason for his discomfort. He seemed surprised when I suggested his fall could have caused it. Horrified, I realized that he had no memory of the accident triggered by his consumption of free alcohol.

Now, it was the third consecutive night that my companion had passed out on the huge bed. Here on the balcony, the slight breeze coming from the ocean cooled my flushed face. What had seemed to be a dream relationship was an illusion. How could I justify the bad decision *to travel with a person I'd known for such a short time? It proved I was a bad judge of character and I needed to distance myself and my emotions from this huge mistake.*

Perhaps I could use this story as a cautionary tale for naïve and hopeful women like me, a warning to others that internet dating wasn't necessarily the solution to being alone.

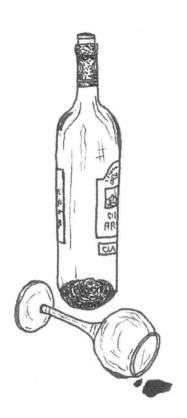

CHAPTER NINETEEN

My stay at Double One Villas coincided with the most important holiday of the Balinese calendar, *Nyepi*, which is equivalent to our New Year's Day. Bali is a nation of ceremonies. It seemed that every day there were ceremonies being held at village temples and family temples. Even the placing of the miniature flower and food baskets in the morning and evening were ceremonies. At Double One Villas, a temple was attached to the wall beside my door. It looked like an ornate birdhouse with its bright orange paint and floral art. Twice a day, a woman, dressed in sarong and sash, placed a new little basket in it. Sometimes, she added a stick of incense that gave off a pungent aroma. I felt blessed by this ritual as though no harm could befall me in my temporary home.

Late in the afternoon of the day before *Nyepi*, our New Year's Eve, all the villages hosted ceremonies and processions. In the preceding days, in many of the villages and in Ubud, I watched men building fantastical, grotesque sculptures. An armature of wood, bamboo sticks and metal rod, held together by wire, established the skeletal forms. Wire mesh gave them shape and paper maché completed the figures. In Ubud, where the figures were larger, their creators fleshed them out with upholsterer's foam or Styrofoam.

These sinister sculptures, called *ogoh-ogoh*, represented the evil spirits that would be driven out of the villages before the New Year began. Neighboring villages competed to build the scariest and largest *ogoh-ogoh*. Grotesque heads, painted with vivid angry colors, sported fangs, protruding eyes and wild, coconut husk hair. Sometimes, small monkey creatures attacked the main figure. Remembering my experience with the thief at the Ubud Monkey Sanctuary, I found this depiction of monkey aggression entirely believable. One sculpture being built in Ubud was over twenty feet tall and had a huge belly painted like a bull's eye with black and yellow paint. Tufts of coconut husk sprouted from the huge eyebrows, from the fingers and from the feet. A web of bamboo poles formed the base of the sculptures and would serve as carrying handles.

Three young men, who were employees or maybe just friends of employees, had asked me if I wanted to go to the *ogoh-ogoh* festivities. Knowing that might entail another harrowing motorcycle drive with a possibly inebriated driver—alcohol is as much a part of *ogoh-ogoh* day as it is on New Year's Eve in the West—I was evasive about my plans.

In the middle of the afternoon, I trudged up the high, stone steps from my little villa abode with my netbook computer to the reception area where WIFI was available. I wondered who would be on duty, Eko or Gede. At first, I couldn't tell them apart. They looked like twin brothers; both were about five feet two inches in height, slightly built, with short, wavy black hair. They took turns on the reception desk, but their shifts were not regular enough to determine who was who. After a few days, I finally figured out that Eko had a barely visible wispy goatee and a dark mole on his chin. Gede wasn't as cheerful as Eko. A constant toothache made him grimace and hold his jaw during conversations. The last time I'd seen him, he had gratefully accepted a few ibuprofen tablets to help deal with the pain.

It was Eko who was on duty.

"Are you going to village for *ogoh-ogoh* ceremony?" he asked.

"I was asked," I said, "but no one has shown up."

"I have friend who drive guests from hotel next door," Eko said. "You go with them."

I abandoned my plans to check my email and hurried back to my room to get my sarong, sash and camera. Just as I returned to the reception area, a minivan rounded the curve on the steep driveway from the adjacent hotel.

"Wayan, stop," Eko yelled to the driver. "This lady want to go too."

"No room," the driver yelled back through the open window.

The van turned onto the main road, and I—crestfallen—started back down the steps of the reception area. The van stopped across the road. It seemed the occupants were holding a conference.

A door opened and a voice said, "We've got room."

I squeezed into the van and discovered that the group consisted of two mother and daughter pairs who were Canadians. Their guide, Wayan, was one of the waiters next door, who I'd already met when I'd eaten lunch there. We were dropped off just outside the village of Culik.

The procession had already started. Groups of boys in matching turbans and t-shirts carried their village's *ogoh-ogoh* on their shoulders. Rhythmic gamelan bands provided a noisy escort accompanied by piecing whistles blown by procession officials. These parade marshals, dressed in distinctive black and white sarongs, attempted to establish some sense of order to the exuberant parade. We joined in at the end with other procession watchers and straggled into the village.

Many people were already sitting cross-legged on the road in neat rows four abreast. The dozen or so Westerners who were standing to watch were invited, in English, by an unseen person far ahead on a public address system, to sit down and participate in the ceremony. I noticed that as the Balinese people in each row sat down they first removed their flip-flops and sat on them. How ingenious, I thought.

Not only does it keep the seat of your sarong clean, but it adds a thin wedge of padding between one's rear end and the hard pavement. The disembodied voice ahead wafted towards us. We took our clues from the people in front of us as to when to clasp our palms together in what I thought might be a Hindi gesture of respect.

It soon became apparent why a walking space had been left down one side of the rows of worshippers. Twice, a priest walked next to the seated mass of people and used a small bamboo whisk to sprinkle us with holy water. I felt honored that I was able to participate in the ceremony and not be just a gawking tourist. The clear side of the street was also used by a dragon character operated by two men with bells on their feet that headed towards the unseen heart of the ceremony far ahead. The return of that mythical creature past us, along with the final sprinkling of holy water, signaled the end of the ceremony.

We followed the crowds to the village crossroads marked in the middle by a stone statue—obviously the centre of the ceremony. Incongruously, a bright lime green dump truck drove up, and men with bamboo mats scooped up all the refuse from the ceremony into the back of the truck. Thousands of carefully woven miniature baskets, loaded with slices of fruit, rice cakes and flowers, were now garbage. I wanted to snatch a little basket at my feet as a souvenir of that special day, but I was afraid it might be sacrilegious to do so.

We had all gathered around the outer edges of the crossroads. Perhaps a thousand people, most from outlying villages, waited four and five deep for darkness to fall. From my vantage point looking at the people around me, I saw that about twenty of them were Westerners. Two tall, middle-aged men stood out, mostly because they towered over the shorter Balinese people. They each had a beautiful young Balinese girl with them, draped in exquisite silk sarongs. I thought they might be the Balinese equivalent of trophy wives.

April 9, 1992

John came by unannounced on Sunday. He had made up his mind.

Tracey wins. He had renewed his relationship with her three weeks ago (which coincided with his change of mind about reconciliation after March Break). She's the opposite of me: younger, outgoing, an extrovert, into sports and athletics, politics and is a planner in the transportation department. He seemed to think I should know her, and I'd never even heard of her. He loves her and she loves him. Again, he said that I made him feel guilty. He is guilty. Why does he dump the blame on me for his own guilt trip?

All of the women were obviously dressed in their best clothes—beautifully colored, patterned sarongs and lacy, long or three-quarter length sleeved blouses worn tight to the body with a form-fitting undergarment. Solid colored sashes, mostly white, defined their waists. Many of the women wore the ubiquitous flips-flops favored by both sexes throughout Bali. The more fashionable or more affluent young women teetered around on high sandals decorated with beads and sequins.

Diminutive grandmothers held squirming babies also clothed in traditional Balinese dress. Most of the spectators were women; the men were either in the parade or parade marshals. Priests, dressed all in white, clung to the sides of the central statue in the middle of the crossroads.

Fireworks and yelling announced the imminent arrival of the first *ogoh-ogoh*. When they arrived at the crossroads, the boys carrying the effigy swooped around the central statue making menacing incursions into the crowd. The crowd fell away from the frightening figure. One of the daughters in our group didn't move out of the way fast enough and was whacked in the shins by a long bamboo carrying pole. She was knocked to the ground and was immediately surrounded by a group of parade marshals who determined that she wasn't badly hurt. For the rest of the parade, the young woman was protected by her mother, who had a firm clasp on her arm, and also by a middle-aged parade marshal who paternally stepped in front of her as each *ogoh-ogoh* swooped close.

The darkness, punctuated by blazing torches carried by boys, the crush of the crowd, the noise and the sense of menace as the monsters came alive through the motions of the boys carrying them, all produced a scene where real danger was possible. The loud crashing sounds were intended to wake up evil spirits and drive them away from the island into the sea.

As part of the throng leaving the crossroads after the parade, I was reminded of a New Year's Eve in Toronto when I was leaving Nathan Phillips Square with an even larger mass of people.

December 31, 1991

The temperature hovered just below freezing, and I wished I'd worn my warmer coat. I was miserable, not only from the cold, but because I was alone. Although part of a crowd of thousands of people, I was one of the few who weren't part of a happy group of friends or family. Taking the streetcar home, I abruptly got off at about the halfway mark and walked for blocks in the piercing cold. I finally reached my goal and began to cry as I looked up at the darkened windows of the house where my children were spending their first New Year's Day apart from me with my newly-estranged husband.

In Bali, I was again surrounded by strangers on the eve of a new year, but my mood was one of sheer joy and thankfulness.

When the procession was over, we walked back to the minivan and climbed in. Driving to our hotels, we were able to witness the last step in the *ogoh-ogoh* carnival. The jubilant and somewhat rowdy sculpture bearers paraded the figures to a gully. One by one, they threw them in and set them on fire. Some of the bolder boys appropriated the more ornate heads and carted them away either as souvenirs or to be sold later to collectors.

Back in front of Double One Villas, the Canadian women asked me to join them at their hotel for a late dinner. It was now eight-thirty in the evening. I said I'd be pleased to join them in a few minutes.

The lobby reception area was dark and I groped unsuccessfully for my room key, which I'd left with Eko before going to the *ogog-ogoh* ceremony.

"Hello, hello, is anybody here?" I called out.

There was no response, but I felt sure there would be someone from the staff down at the dining area. It, too, was in darkness. There was no sign, either, of Lily, the only other guest. The place was deserted, and I was locked out of my room.

I climbed the steps to my porch and noticed the two windows on either side of the door. It was lucky I abhorred air conditioning. Rather than use it, I'd opened both windows to allow air to flow into my room. The windows extended down to within a foot of the floor. They were hinged at the top and opened outward, awning-style. Two metal rods held them open. I unhooked the rods, lifted the window outward and was relieved when it opened wide enough for me to crawl in. Finding it so easy to break into my own room, I realized that diligently locking my door each time I left wasn't going to keep my possessions safe unless I also closed and locked the windows. From then on, feeling no sense of danger, I saw no need to lock the door whether I was in my room or not.

I joined the women next door.

"Which one of you lovely ladies am I sleeping with tonight?" I said.

Seeing their stricken faces, I relented and told them I was late because I'd been locked out and had to figure out how to break into my room. I was glad they'd asked me to join them for dinner; their hotel staff had not jumped ship like mine. It was long past my normal dinner time, and after the excitement of the day's events, I was hungry.

The next morning, Lily was at breakfast when I arrived in the dining area.

"Oh, I'm so glad to see you," she said. "When I came back from the *ogoh-ogoh* ceremony, your room was dark, and I couldn't find any of the staff. I was worried about you."

I told her about going to the ceremony and what happened when I got back. It was nice to find out that I was missed by someone.

"Thanks for thinking of me," I said.

Lily was a tall, big-boned, blond Australian woman in her mid-to-late sixties. She appeared to be well known and liked by the staff. She wore loose, long dresses that helped to hide the compression stockings on her legs. The tight stockings, which ended at her ankles, accentuated the swollen mass of her feet. The heat and humidity in Bali made her legs and feet balloon to a huge size.

"I was in the bungalow next to you," she said. "When Eko told me you were very quiet and always writing in a notebook, I asked him to move me further down the hill."

She seemed flustered by her confession.

"I don't want you to think I was trying to get away from you," she said. "I was thinking about your work. Your need for peace and quiet."

"It wouldn't have been a problem," I said. "You should have heard the crickets, frogs and roosters where I stayed before."

"Ah," she said, "you don't know my friends. My Balinese friends. They're around all the time. It gets very noisy."

I told her the previous night's abandonment by the staff had provided more peace and quiet than I needed.

Chapter Twenty

Bali is basically closed for business on *Nyepi*. Even the airport is closed. *Nyepi* is called the day of silence. Music, radio and other such noisy distractions are not allowed; even couples are forbidden from indulging in the activity that would seem a good match for a quiet day. The use of electricity is frowned upon, and the most serious devotees don't eat or talk but meditate or do yoga. Special security guards, *pecaleng*, patrol the streets to ensure that everybody obeys the strict rules. The Balinese believe silence will force the evil spirits to leave in search of noise.

The rules allow hotels to feed their guests, but guests may not leave the property. I told Eko that I planned to visit my new Canadian friends next door.

He looked at me, horrified. "You can't," he said.

"Why not?"

"Hotel fined if guest on road."

"I won't be on the road," I assured him. "I'll walk on the beach."

I was writing on my porch when one of the female staff dropped by to invite me down to the dining area for a complimentary drink to celebrate *Nyepi*. It sounded similar to the invitation to the Captain's cocktail party that one receives on a cruise ship. I didn't go right away since ten-thirty in the morning was a little early to have a celebratory drink. Soon a man came to reissue the invitation. I didn't want to insult my hosts, so I dutifully trotted down the stone steps to the dining area. Five young men, seated cross-legged on the floor, gestured for me to join them. One of them poured a glass of Bintang beer from one of several large bottles on the floor nearby and handed it to me. Another man offered me a cigarette, which I declined, and we settled in to celebrate the New Year.

I'm not usually a beer drinker so it seemed strange to be sipping beer, sitting cross-legged on the floor with five young male strangers, only one of whom spoke much English. Mostly, we exchanged smiles and stared at the packages of cigarettes and ashtrays in the circle in front of us. The man beside me reached into the circle for a small bowl of what appeared to be barbequed chicken bones and held it in front of me. I accepted a piece and gnawed a miniscule morsel of meat from the bone.

A man in the circle got up and retrieved a bowl of fruit—apples and snakefruit.

"We grow many apples in Canada," I said, trying desperately to find something to talk about with these silent men.

I picked up one of the apples. There was a barcode sticker on the apple, and I fully expected to see Canada printed on it. I could barely make out the small print that said USA.

"Wow," I said. "This apple has come all the way from the United States."

"Not from there," said the only man who spoke English. "Label just there to impress. These from Indonesia."

I'd noticed during the ceremonial procession the previous day how many apples with similar labels were included in the baskets or offerings carried by the women on their heads. Apples as a form of fake status symbol; not what you would have expected in Bali.

One of the young men in the circle had an unusually large and elaborate dragon tattoo across his back and down one arm. It was this man who took an apple and meticulously peeled it, taking his time, dividing it into small sections, inspecting each piece carefully. Finally, satisfied that he had a worthy offering, he presented the bowl to me, holding it out between us, locking his eyes on mine. What he lacked in English, he made up for with his nonverbal communication skills. I thought of the apple Eve presented to Adam.

I attempted to pass the bowl around, but the men indicated that they would eat later. After a respectable length of time, I excused myself, thanked them and retreated to my porch. Later, when I questioned Lily about it, she said that Western women were invited to "drink with the boys," but Balinese women were not. I wondered if our status was somehow higher than the Balinese women or if it was just assumed that I could afford to buy a round of beer. On that front, I'm sure I'd been a disappointment. I was to find out later that I was a disappointment on many fronts.

Each of our hotels had different rules concerning *Nyepi*. At mine, Eko informed me, dinner would be served between five and six. At three-fifteen, while I was working on my porch, the waiter from the dining pavilion came by.

"We put rice on now."

"This is too early for dinner," I said. "I'll be down at five."

Lily joined me for dinner. On the dot of six, our waiter said that the staff was leaving. They were going to the staffroom, which they called the mess.

"We are here from early morning," he said.

I learned from Lily that the skeleton staff had brought their children with them early that day, before six, for the official start of *Nyepi*. All of them, including the children, would be staying overnight at the hotel until the six o'clock close of *Nyepi* the next morning.

After dinner, I picked my way along the rocky beach, careful to duck my head under the outrigger arms of the *jukung* lining the shore. To my surprise, all the lights were on at Wawa Wewe II, the hotel restaurant next door. I call it a restaurant, but it would be more accurate to describe it as a covered outdoor patio. My friends had just been served their meals. A little boy, the son of the waitress, slept on a makeshift bed assembled out of two chairs and some cushions.

Just before eight o'clock, the waitress came to our table.

"We close now. You leave," she said.

"Can we have the lights on in our rooms?" one of my companions asked.

"No lights. No noise. *Nyepi* not finish," she replied.

"Come to my room," one of the daughters said. "We can watch a movie on my laptop. The battery's all charged."

Such are the miracles of modern technology that the temporary lack of electricity wouldn't deprive these women of their digital entertainment.

"Goodnight," I said. "Enjoy your movie."

Back in my room, I stealthily turned on the bedside lamp and hoped that I wouldn't be caught using the dim little light. I needed to record the events of the day while they were still fresh in my mind. I looked up at the rotating fan and wondered if the women next door would be allowed to use their air conditioners. In many villages, they turn off the electricity to ensure the rules of *Nyepi* are followed. I noticed light coming from the open door of the staff mess and heard the murmur of voices. It seemed that silent day for the staff in the hotels wasn't observed as stringently as in the villages.

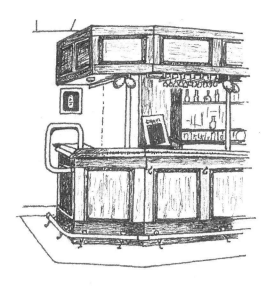

Chapter Twenty-One

During my stay at Double One Villas, staff members frequently asked how long I was staying. I think it was because all of them wanted to arrange a driver for me when I left. Driving seemed to be the major source of income, and whoever arranged the drive would get a commission. Whenever I took a walk on the road, within about five minutes, at least six men on motorbikes would ask if I needed a ride. During my whole time in Bali, I was never offered driving services by a woman. Whether women were not encouraged to be entrepreneurial, or whether it was a cultural constraint, I didn't know.

February 1997

I drove slowly up the street again. Had I missed the building on my first pass? My friend Nancy had been excited when she told me about the small commercial building she saw on a side street running north from the Lakeshore. The profusion of one-way streets in the neighborhood confused her; she had discovered it by mistake. It was for sale.

It was dark, and the scum of salt stains on my car windows made it hard to see out. The skuzzy-grey piles of snow could have swallowed up the FOR SALE sign. Nancy had been definite—the boxy, two-story building sat between two red brick bungalows on Fifth Street, just north of the commercial retail area.

Could that be it? It matched Nancy's description, but where was the FOR SALE sign? I pulled my car over as close to the curb as possible against the hard icy snow furrow thrown up by a snow plow. Searching for a realtor's sign in the unshoveled snow in front of the building, I noticed the front door, crudely constructed from plywood, the crumbling stucco on the lower story and the general air of abandonment. Finally, I found a weather-beaten sign in an obscure position on the second floor wall and scribbled the barely visible phone number on the back of a parking lot receipt. This building looked so bad, I might actually be able to buy it.

"If that girl buys that building, she ought to have her head examined!"

My mother nervously reported my father's words after they'd driven by the building. He'd been less than impressed by the derelict look of the place. The unkempt state of the bungalow next door, with its peeling paint and an assortment of junk poking through the snow piles on the front lawn—and the general down-at-the-heels aura of the neighborhood—reinforced his opinion that my decision to sell a perfectly good house to buy an abandoned banquet hall/former Steel Worker's Union Hall was idiotic. My children advanced guesses as to how long it would be before Grumpy, their name for my father, would speak to me again. It turned out to be four months. By that time, I'd sold my house, and he realized, if only for his grandchildren's sake, that he had to begrudgingly accept my decision and help us convert the banquet hall into a home.

We stepped over piles of curled, stained flyers and unopened mail that had been pushed through the mail slot to the left of the door. The real estate agent had a flashlight. A colleague had warned her that the electricity had been shut off when the building's owners had gone bankrupt. The oil bills had not been paid either, so we could see our breath in the dim winter light struggling to come through the filthy windows.

The room at ground level, located near the front door, looked as though it had been abandoned in mid-renovation. New drywall had been attached to most of the walls, but the seams had not been taped or plastered. We left footprints in the thick layer of dust on the plywood floor as we maneuvered our way around piles of construction debris, discarded coffee cups, a shop vacuum and an obviously useless portable electric heater.

In spite of the unfinished, chaotic state of the room, I saw its potential as an art gallery. There was immediate access to it from the front door. The three, tall, skinny windows, once cleaned, would bring in just enough natural light. And wonder of wonders, the ceiling was twelve feet high! The relatively uninterrupted wall space would be perfect for hanging art.

Six steps up, and down a hallway, was a reception room, men and women's washrooms and a small kitchen. The building had been converted, a few years back, from a union hall into an Irish Social Club. The impractical owners had obtained a substantial loan from the bank for renovations prior to applying for a permanent liquor license. It was denied, and the owners attempted to recoup some of their money by renting out the place for the occasional private party. The last such party had been a stag.

My father had been appalled by the outside condition of the building; he would have been disgusted by the disarray of the interior. Even the backyard of the building was a wasteland. As the snow melted in the spring, it revealed a muddy expanse of weeds dotted by broken bottles, beer bottle caps and other garbage.

Inside, the middle-level rooms and hallway, littered with booze and beer bottles and the occasional condom wrapper, looked and smelled like a garbage dump. A moldy, green carpet patterned by cigarette burns, butts and plaster dust, covered the floor. A glass door, presumably the one that had been replaced by the crude plywood one, leaned up against a stove covered in mouse turds and grease. Open cupboard doors revealed blue and ochre commercial quality dinner plates, side plates and cups and saucers, all coated in dust and bits of dried food. Splatters of vomit crusted the washroom sinks and floors, and soiled paper towels spilled from an upturned waste bin.

I saw potential under the filth and the garbage. Taking down a few walls would create a spacious studio space. The kitchen sink would serve as a studio sink, and the cupboards could store my art supplies. By removing the sinks and toilets from the women's washroom, the plumbing could be used to convert the space into an acid room/clean-up room. With the removal of the urinals from the men's washroom—although my son Andrew argued to leave one of them for his use—the conversion of one of the toilet stalls to a shower and the removal of the enclosure walls and doors from the other toilet stall, the room could be transformed into a proper bathroom.

My heart pounded as we climbed the stairs to the second floor. On the other side of a metal fire door was one big room. Facing us was an eighteen foot long English pub bar. A tarnished brass foot rail ran along the length of the bar, and equally tarnished brass posts held up a cupboard with wine glass holders attached to the bottom of it. A few wine glasses were still hanging there, but most of them were scattered over the bar counter and on banquet tables. Chairs with chrome legs and black plastic padded seats were stacked in a niche near the door. The lower half of the wall was paneled with the same walnut-stained wood as the bar. It was even darker up here than on the lower floors because opaque, green Plexiglas covered the windows. A soiled green carpet covered the whole floor except for a small wood parquet dancing area in front of a platform that had evidently been used for either a disc jockey or a small band.

This would be our apartment.

When he first saw the building, my son thought it was cool, especially when he learned that a room in the basement, filled with old tires, a gigantic office safe and a motley collection of office furniture, could be renovated to create a private bachelor pad for him.

My daughter's response was to break into tears and say she wanted to live with her father. "There's no bathroom up here, no bedrooms, and there's not even a proper kitchen," she sobbed.

I tried to reassure her. "We can put big sliding doors in that end for two sleeping areas and a bathroom with glass block walls to let the light through."

"But I want bedrooms and a bathroom with real walls. I don't want people to see me sitting on the toilet!"

I wanted Alison to live with me, so I modified my grandiose but impractical vision of a completely open apartment. The beer cooler—another feature my son thought we should keep—and the bar shelves, backed by smoked-glass mirrors, were replaced by conventional kitchen cupboards, a proper sink, stove and refrigerator. A friend who was an architect drew up plans for the interior so that the blueprints would meet building code requirements. His plan included a kitchen island, a design feature of homes at that time. It was to replace the mammoth bar.

"Paul, that's one of the reasons I bought this place. The bar adds such a funky vibe; it's part of its history."

In the end, we compromised. Two-thirds of the bar stayed, complete with the wine glass racks and brass foot rails and hat hooks. In deference to Alison, "real walls" enclosed two bedrooms and a bathroom. The crowning jewel of the space was a nine-foot-square, pyramidal skylight built by a commercial skylight maker. "Bruce the Moose," as we nicknamed him, agreed to construct it even though my building wasn't his typical shopping mall project. He said he admired my moxie for transforming the ugly-duckling building into a unique home, studio and art gallery.

CHAPTER TWENTY-TWO

For at least the first week in Amed, I had trouble figuring out who were staff members and who were just friends of staff. Unexpectedly, most of them started wearing shirts made from the same patterned fabric that finally identified them as official staff. Maybe that first week all the shirts were out being washed at the same time. The number of staff appeared to be huge considering that this place had only ten units, and for a few nights, I was the only guest. I found out that there were sixteen employees, although not all of them worked at the same time. No wonder I was having such a hard time learning names.

It should have been easy to learn their names as there were only four first names in Bali depending on birth order. The first child born was named Wayan, the second Made, then Nyoman (the one I had the hardest time pronouncing) and Ketut. If more children were born, the fifth would be Wayan Oops! the person joked who was explaining this naming scheme. The sixth would be Made and so on. There was no common last name. When their babies were about three months old, parents gave them second names based on what they would like them to be when they were adults or a name based on characteristic traits the babies displayed. One of the waiter/cooks was named Made Kuah. He was the second child, and his parents hoped he would be a cook, so his second name meant "broth." Male names began with an "I" and female names with "Ni," but these prefixes were not used in conversation. To further confuse matters, some people introduced themselves using their second names or even nicknames instead of their first names.

After a few days at Double One Villas, one of the reception staff told me that the credit card machine didn't work and I would have to pay in cash. My bill was adding up by this time, since I was also buying some of my lunches and dinners there.

Suki, the hard-bargaining young man who had taken me snorkeling, overheard this exchange. He offered to drive me—for a fee, of course—to the nearest town with an ATM machine. This was at Amlapura, a town in the mountains we had passed through on the way to Amed. Suki was a serious man, unsmiling and unwilling to compromise on a price for his transport services. His sales method was to say that it was up to me to decide what to pay, and when it came time to pay, he tried to double or triple the amount I offered him.

For the trip to the ATM machine, which he said was a round trip of about two hours, I negotiated the trip price ahead of time. I offered him fifty thousand rupiah, about six dollars. I thought this was a reasonable offer, considering that Lily had told me the average daily income of the local people was one dollar. He agreed, and to sweeten the deal, he offered to bring helmets for the ride, which he would borrow from a friend. I knew my family at home would appreciate my wearing a helmet. What I didn't realize until later was that helmets were mandatory in Bali. There were no police in this backwater fishing village so very few people wore helmets. There *were* police in Amlapura where we were going, and they made regular spot checks for helmets and fined people who were not wearing them.

He suggested wearing a shirt with long sleeves and long pants. In my paranoia, I wondered if these were the Balinese equivalent to bikers wearing "leathers" to protect themselves.

At the appointed time, we met beside his motorbike. He handed me a helmet and finally helped me with the fastener on the chin strap when I had trouble doing it up. He said I didn't need the chin strap, but I insisted; I had visions of lying on the road without a helmet. Putting it on reminded me of putting on my hockey helmet. Unlike that helmet, which had a metal wire cage, this motorcycle helmet had a clear visor. Good, I thought, my face will be protected too.

The road next to the coast hugged the water in some places and rose in others to skirt the numerous coves. Rather than closing my eyes, or looking ahead, I decided that the least scary view was to the side. That way, if we ran over a rooster or hit a pedestrian, I wouldn't see it coming. A few less roosters mightn't have been a great loss. I soon learned that I had to lean back slightly so that my helmet wasn't clanking into Suki's helmet. The road ran through three villages that passed in a blur. So much for trying to sightsee.

We turned off the coastal road onto a slightly wider road with fewer potholes and washed-out areas. As we climbed the mountains, turning first one way and then another, the road skirting the side of the mountain like a tangled rope, I felt a few drops of rain. Following the example of other motorcycle drivers, Suki pulled to the side and removed a rain cape from his storage area under the seat. I was glad I'd brought a rain cape as well. I pulled it out of the bag I wore on my back. Suki's cape was grey with discrete yellow safety tape on the back. Mine was screaming fluorescent orange, an ancient rain cape from my daughter's stay at summer camp. Before I left Canada, I'd patched several jagged tears with duct tape. For some reason, it was missing a one-foot-square section from a corner. One set of snaps used to keep the cape together was gone.

As I attempted to put my rain cape over the helmet, Suki suggested with a note of impatience that I had to take the helmet off first.

"Put hood up. Then helmet," he said. "Forget chin strap."

"No way," I said.

Suki reminded me of my son, almost the same age, who played hockey without doing up his chin strap, magically believing the helmet would stay on his head no matter how rough the game was. I was beginning to feel like a mother dealing with a sullen teenager. He acted as if he could barely tolerate my incompetence, something my real son did occasionally. Taking on this mother/son role made me feel more comfortable as it was a familiar one. This was my Balinese son, and we would have to put up with each other.

Monday, May 1, 1992

A good day today! Andrew to school, drove to Canadian Tire, fixed barbeque cover and lawnmower, mowed lawn, biked to Barb's, listened to tapes while embroidering, did little bit of plate work, planted peas, dug garden, no naps and lots of energy.

Positive Reinforcement tapes—I like myself, I like myself, I like myself. I am responsible for myself; I like myself. Learn to forgive people, parents, relationships, etc. We control our own emotions. Concept of guilt—not quite what I agree with. Guilt is not given to someone by someone else; it is something the person feels themselves. Negative criticism is source of low self-esteem. Relaxation and meditation with classical music reinforces goals. Write out goals on cards.

I am a good artist.

I will make a living with my art.

I will not be afraid of failure.

Visualize the worst possible outcome and then work to prevent it. Positive visualization of goals. Used in athletics to program body to positive outcome and reaching of goals.

I am responsible for myself.

I am a good mother.

I am not a boring person.

I am an intelligent person.

Pleased with my choice of camera. Look into fares to Vancouver and phone tourist bureau for info.

I like myself.

I will not allow myself to be manipulated.

I like myself and can live without John's approval. He loves someone else because of his own shortcomings and ego gratification rather than because I am a failure. I am capable of making my own decisions and have always been competent in running the household. I have created a good home and a beautiful garden.

I will succeed.

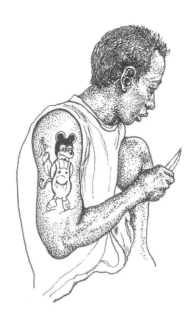

Chapter Twenty-Three

The rain made our ride dangerous. I tried to remember if my travel insurance stipulated that it wouldn't cover injuries sustained in motorcycle accidents. Statistics citing that most tourist accidents involved motorcycles flashed through my mind. When I'm in a stressful situation, I ask myself the question, what's the worst that can happen? My answer now was that getting killed was preferable to being injured. I decided that praying to both my Christian God and the local Hindu gods wouldn't do any harm. I was hoping that all the evil spirits, including the demon responsible for motorcycle accidents, had been driven from the island during the exhortation ceremonies the evening of the *ogoh-ogoh* procession.

At one crossroad, I noticed the sign to Amlapura pointed to the right and we went to the left. Suki must have opted for the longer "scenic route" since in the end we arrived in Amlapura. Suki made a purchase at a store and I made my withdrawal at the ATM machine.

Knowing that I now had lots of money, Suki tried to pull the ruse that the negotiated fare had been for a one-way trip, not a return trip. Unusually for me, I didn't fall for this ploy and emphasized that we had negotiated a return trip and that I wouldn't be paying him until we arrived back at Double One Villas. He accepted this with a shrug, probably thinking, "Nothing ventured, nothing gained."

The monsoon started as we climbed up into the mountains. Rain lashed us and rivulets flowed from Suki's helmet down my neck into the gap left by the cape. My pant legs were soon soaked since the rain cape didn't cover them. My visor fogged up from the inside and that, along with the torrent of water on the outside of the visor, almost totally obscured my vision. I could just barely make out the rivers flowing at the edges of the road. Although my vision was minimal, I hoped that Suki's visor was clear. He must have been able to see because he lifted his feet as we approached the ponds accumulating in low points of the road.

Perhaps he could feel my panic from the grip of my knees on his legs and the squeeze of my hands on his waist. Out of character, he asked, "You okay?"

"Yes," I stuttered through clenched teeth.

I'd come to Bali for adventure, but this wasn't what I had in mind.

All the gods in heaven, both Christian and Hindu, must have been listening to my prayers because we arrived back at Double One Villas soaked but safe. Suki showed me his hands, which he said were cramped from grasping the handles of the motorcycle. Our soggy ride hadn't been easy for him either.

Seeing a more vulnerable side of Suki's personality encouraged me to ask him about his name.

"Are you Wayan, Made, Nyoman, or Ketut?" I asked.

"Made," he said.

"Why did your parents call you Suki?"

He gestured towards his motorcycle. "Suki short for Suzuki." They had great hopes that their son would eventually own a motorcycle.

"But why do your friends call you Miki?"

He lifted up his rain cape and the edge of his t-shirt sleeve and pointed to a tattoo on his right bicep. There was Mickey Mouse but not the benign Disney version. This Mickey was a diabolical mouse, all swagger and attitude—a dangerous mouse—one to be cautious of.

Chapter Twenty-Four

Dinner by candlelight one evening wasn't planned. Having ordered my food, I was enjoying the fading light that bathed the ocean and clouds in tones of pearly grey. The ocean was black at the horizon with lighter bands of silver closer to the shore. Booms echoed from clouds passing over the mountains. As one such boom sounded, the lights went out.

Made brought several tealight candles to my table.

"Made, the generator will be working soon, like last night, right?" I asked. There had been a similar blackout the night before.

"Not like last night," he replied. "No one here to start motor. My friend come. Maybe half hour."

He lit the tiny candles. The flames flickered in the breeze, at times threatening to go out.

It was March 7, Andrew's birthday, and I ordered extravagantly to celebrate his birthday in absentia. Before the lights went out, I tried ordering a glass of Balinese red wine from Made, but the only wine available was Balinese white wine in a cardboard box. I searched the drinks menu for another celebratory drink. A Bloody Mary was exotic enough, I thought. I conferred with Made, who had to call to the cook to determine whether they had the necessary ingredients. Yes, they had vodka, but they had no idea what the ingredient listed as "Leaparin" was. They were both in vigorous agreement that Tabasco was available. That, I turned down, thinking of my sensitive stomach. The drink, when it arrived, was an interesting variation on a Bloody Mary. Vodka seemed to be the main ingredient although I suspected the "vodka" was the locally made moonshine, *arak*. A fresh tomato was pureed in a blender with the alcohol, and a slice of tomato decorated the edge of the glass. This was a creative interpretation of a Bloody Mary. By the time it arrived, the lights had just gone out (maybe the electric blender used to make the drink had caused the blackout), and the pink blush color of the drink looked interesting in the candlelight. Although I didn't want the Tabasco, they must have used some because I began sneezing after taking a sip of the spicy drink.

I ordered grilled prawns with a garlic sauce, blowing caution to the wind as far as my meal budget was concerned. Made assured me that the meal could still be prepared without electricity. Perhaps they used a propane stove. Eating unshelled prawns, presented head and all, is a challenge at the best of times, but in the meager light, it was a major effort to separate the meat from the shell and head. The effects of the Bloody Mary reduced my dexterity with a knife and fork. I abandoned the utensils and used my fingers. A large portion of lightly sautéed garlic accompanied the prawns. Vampires would be no threat to me that evening. I hoped the garlic had a similar repelling effect on mosquitoes.

I wanted to have cake for dessert, thinking of it as my son's birthday cake. There was none listed on the menu. I asked Made for the yogurt with honey and fruit that *was* listed. There was no yogurt. I asked for the flambé bananas with lime and ice cream. There was no ice cream. As a last ditch effort, I asked for the black rice pudding. I was rewarded for my persistence with a bowl of lovely, sweet pudding embellished with a swirl of something that might have been coconut cream. The pudding was loaded with calories that I knew I would regret consuming, but in honor of Andrew's birthday, it was a warranted indulgence.

As Made served the fattening dessert, the lights came back on. I could now see people at two of the other tables. Maybe I could persuade them to sing Happy Birthday in honor of my son and we could blow out the candles on our tables. This would have been a nice gesture, but I didn't want them to question my sanity. I'd celebrated my son's birth alone in my own way. He was in my thoughts and, more importantly, he was in my heart.

"Ding-dong, ding-dong, dong-dong-ding-dong."

The door bell chiming its Big Ben melody interrupted my inking of a small copper etching plate. Not taking the time to remove the inky plastic gloves to press the 'open' button on the intercom in my studio, I instead walked down the hall to the front door. I was startled to see a police officer standing outside the glass door.

"Does Andrew Livey live here?" he intoned in a deep, officious voice.
My stomach churned and my heart raced.

"Yes, no," I stuttered. "I mean, yes, this is his home, but no, he's not living here at the moment. He's living in Kingston and attending the Royal Military College. I'm his mother. Has something happened?"

I feared the worst; why else would a police officer be asking for him? He'd had several misadventures in the last few years, the most recent of which was a serious head injury from a bar room brawl in Kingston. The resulting concussion, coming as it did after several other previous concussions, acquired both on and off the ice, had ended his hockey-playing career on the RMC team almost before it started.

"We've had a call from the Kingston police that a license plate from a car registered in his name was found last night at the end of a bridge over a canal connecting the RMC campus with the mainland. The guardrail was damaged and there's a possibility that the car might have gone into

the water."

"I'm sorry, I have to sit down." I sank down to sit on the top step of the stairs leading from the front foyer.

"Do you have a number in Kingston where we can try to reach him?" Seeing my pale face and stricken look, the officer's voice had softened somewhat.

With shaking hands, I dialed the telephone number at the apartment my son shared with a friend.

"Tyler and Andrew aren't here. Leave a message." The message on the answering machine was brief.

"Andrew, this is your mother. Call me as soon as you get this message." I hung up the phone and stared blankly at the officer, not knowing what to do next. I jumped when the phone rang.

"Hey, Ma. What's up? Your message sounded kind of funny."

"Andrew, are you all right?" I blurted.

"Sure."

"I've got a police officer here who thinks your car went off a bridge."

There was a pause on the end of the line.

"Well, Ma," he said, "on my way back from playing cards with the guys last night, my tires hit a patch of ice on the approach to the bridge. I skidded into the guard rail. There was hardly any damage to the car or rail so I didn't report it. How did they know it was my car that dinged the rail?"

"I guess you don't know you left your license plate behind?"

My voice was curt. My initial fear, and then relief at knowing he was safe, had given way to anger.

Chapter Twenty-Five

After a week at Double One Villas, I seemed to have been adopted by Suki. We assumed the roles of Canadian mother and Balinese son. I appeared to be his major source of income. He either hung around the reception area or the beach all day with occasional visits to my porch or to the table in the reception area where I used the WIFI. He asked if I could help him get an email address. I cited my incompetence with computers as a reason for not being the best person to help him. Eventually, as I learned to use my new netbook computer, my skills improved, and I helped him open a Gmail account. The same day, Eko, who was working at the reception desk, asked if I could help input credit card information a guest had left as payment for her bill. When I'd been told earlier that the machine wasn't working, it was really a matter of Eko and Gede not knowing how to use it. Together, we figured it out and I felt useful.

Teaching art, not full-time but for short contracts, was one of the ways I earned income. One of my most challenging gigs was at a shelter for homeless youths. For one day a week, over the period of a month, I came to the shelter to teach as part of the day program. One of the criteria for being able to stay at the shelter was that the residents, who were between sixteen and twenty-four, had to attend school, have a job or participate in the day program. This rule was intended to teach them useful skills and keep them occupied and out of trouble. Since they had no choice about attending the day program, some were less than enthusiastic about being there.

"Come on, Darren." The youth worker cajoled the lanky young man sprawled in an armchair in the lounge. "The art teacher's here, and since she's doing the day program, you have to do it."

Darren hardly looked up from texting on his cell phone to respond in a sulky tone, "I don't do no art. What's it good for?"

Indeed, I thought, how is learning to stencil a design on a t-shirt going to help any of these kids cope with the problems in their lives that had led to them living in a homeless shelter? Two tough-looking girls with multiple piercings, hoodies and impossibly tight jeans sauntered into the small eating area, deliberately avoiding eye contact with me. It took at least ten minutes for the motley group to assemble in the cramped dining room that served as an improvised art studio.

"Larissa, you know you can't listen to your ipod during day program. Darren, either put your phone away or you'll have to give it to me." The staff member attempted to focus the group's attention on me.

The four boys in the group were wearing outdoor jackets and ball caps as though their attendance here was only temporary, which for one boy it was. A few in the group appeared to be interested as I explained that they would be designing their own logos. I would then show them how to stencil their designs onto a t-shirt. As they worked on designing their personal logos, I could see certain themes emerging. The girls drew their initials surrounded by flowers and hearts. The boys' designs included knives dripping blood, rock band logos and the distinctive leaf shape of the marijuana plant.

"Miss, I can't do this. I don't know how to draw. This is stupid." Darren stared defiantly at me with the blank sheet of paper in front of him.

This was going to be a long day.

At the lunch break, the shelter supervisor called me into her office.

"Did you count your exacto knives before you started?" she asked. "You've got two slashers in that group."

Stunned, I replied, "Yes, I did. Do they slash themselves or other people?"

"You've got one of each."

At the end of the day, as I was counting my exacto knives and putting away all the supplies that I'd brought with me, a boy who had worked silently and separately from the rest of the group approached me. He had struggled with drawing his logo and with cutting the paper stencil.

In a soft voice, so he wouldn't be overheard by any of the others, he said, "Thank you for coming. I learned a lot."

CHAPTER TWENTY-SIX

Suki asked at least once a day about driving me back to the cove where the Japanese shipwreck was located. It was a lucrative drive for him because he had made about twelve dollars on our first trip. This amount included acting as my snorkel guide. During that first trip, he didn't seem comfortable being in the water. Subsequently, Lily told me that very few Balinese people know how to swim and they didn't go in the ocean because it was an evil force and the home of evil spirits. The ocean was where the evil spirits represented by the *ogoh-ogoh* had been driven on the eve of *Nyepi*. Incredibly, most of the fishermen didn't know how to swim.

Realizing that I didn't want to go back to the shipwreck cove so soon, he tried a different approach. "I take you to *warung*. Nice food. Very cheap."

I was open to trying a new place to eat, so off we went on his motorbike.

"Shall I take my orange fluorescent rain cape?" I said, teasing him.

He looked up at the sky over the mountains. "No rain tonight," he replied seriously.

The *warung* was a ten-minute ride away. The building was right beside the road and open on two sides, a typical Balinese style of architecture. We were the only customers, so I could see why they needed our business. I ordered a small bottle of beer and asked Suki if he would like one. He suggested that we could share a large one, and I appreciated his gesture to save money. I ordered grilled snapper; he ordered grilled barracuda. We settled in to enjoy the tasty meal.

Having dinner with Suki felt like an awkward first date. Suki's grasp of English was rudimentary, so the conversation was choppy and basic. He had completed grade nine; his parents couldn't afford to keep him in school to grade twelve. His favorite subjects in school were English and drawing, particularly landscapes. We had found a common interest but exhausted the subject of landscape drawing rather quickly. His parents were corn farmers nearby.

Suki, like many young people everywhere, was constantly text messaging on his cell phone.

"Are you texting a girlfriend?" I asked.

"No, sister," he replied.

He said his sister worked in a town at a considerable distance from Amed. His sister was married and had a son. His sister's husband had taken a second wife, which Lily had earlier told me was fairly common in Bali. His sister and the second wife didn't get along, and his sister had left her husband's family compound. Unfortunately, for the women who leave their husbands or are divorced, the children always stay with the father.

The coach of the Humber Valley Indians came out of the boys' dressing room after the final practice of the season to talk to the parents waiting outside.

"Don't forget that next week's ice time is for our father-and-son scrimmage."

As a newly single hockey mom, I'd been silently fuming since the coach announced this annual end-of-season ritual a few weeks before. Since then, I'd mulled over the unfairness of excluding mothers, especially those of us who had taken on the responsibility of being the sole chauffeur, schlepping our sons to rinks all over the city during the six-month hockey season. Normally, I wasn't an assertive person, but I was wounded and angry about my husband's recent abandonment.

I piped up nervously, "Can Moms play too?"

Shocked faces, especially those of the fathers who were present, turned to see who had suggested this heresy that interfered with a long tradition.

"Can Sarah play, too? Shouldn't this be a family game?" Another mom, whose older daughter played hockey, came to my support.

Silently, I thanked her for supporting my crazy idea. It was a crazy idea as I'd never played hockey with a group of active eleven-to-twelve-year-old boys and their equally competitive fathers. In fact, I'd never played hockey at all except for the occasional skate with my children on our backyard mini rink.

The coach considered the question and finally agreed that it would be a family game, probably thinking that none of the mothers would have the courage or the skill to participate. As the boys straggled out of the dressing room, he advised them of the newly named family game. He didn't provide a reason for the change or say who instigated the idea, so I was spared the agony of embarrassing my son.

All that week, I worried about following through on my proposal. I'd been successful about making a point about an inclusive game, but did I need to actually do it, perhaps with the result of really embarrassing my son? Although supporting me in principle, my daughter didn't want to join me, unwilling to make a fool of herself. She had never played hockey either. At least one of us was thinking rationally.

"Ma, do you shoot right or left?" I think my son realized the potential for trouble when he saw my blank look.

"Never mind; just use this one." He thrust a stick at me.

I knew I was in trouble the moment I stepped onto the ice wearing my twenty-five-year-old, no-longer-white figure skates. The boys wore full equipment—helmets with metal face guards, shoulder pads, elbow

127

pads, padded pants, neck guards, shin pads — the whole shebang. My protective equipment amounted to a bulky hand-knit toque with a multicolored pompom on top.

A compassionate dad gestured to where I should place myself for the face-off. Sheepishly, I took my position. I should have known where to stand having watched my son play hockey from the age of five.

The game was on!

The most competitive kid on the team, although small in size, was a fast skater. He carried the puck down the ice straight towards me. When it looked as though impact was imminent, he skillfully deked around me, which was fairly easy to do considering that I hadn't moved from the spot I was in at the time of the face-off. Luckily, our goalie blocked his shot. It was time for me to move. The puck was in the corner closest to me. Digging in the pick on the blade of my figure skate, I raced, or more accurately, slowly glided to the corner, with my hockey stick held awkwardly in front of me. Just as I touched the puck, the biggest player on the team reached the same spot.

As I tried to get up from my prone position on the ice, my son came to my defense.

"Hey, Gerald, that was my mom you just knocked down!"

My hockey debut resulted in a very sore bum, but the principle I'd sacrificed my dignity for was put into practice.

Suki was twenty-nine and said he didn't have a girlfriend. "I look for Western woman," he said over dinner.

"Why a Western woman?"

"No money to marry Balinese woman. Need good job."

"What would be a good job?" I asked.

"Work in hotel."

"Doing what?"

He put down the cell phone he'd been texting on.

"Waiter," he said. "That good job."

Obviously, for him, being self-employed as a driver and guide, particularly in the low season, was *not* a good job.

I paid our bill, which was the equivalent of about twelve dollars, and off we roared back to the villas.

Getting off the bike, I asked Suki if he would like some money for driving me.

He patted his stomach. "No," he said. "You feed me."

I should have known that something was awry inside the building by the evidence on the outside. Streams and gobs of a glistening, mucous-like material adorned the second floor windows, the upper story brick wall and were indelibly embedded in the stucco on the lower half of the wall. Shards of brown glass littered the sidewalk.

Oh, oh, I thought, as I came down the hallway to the space that would eventually be my studio. The sledge hammers weren't where we had left them. As I rounded the corner into the room, I saw why. One of the sledge hammers my son and his friend had been using before the weekend was lying on the floor beside a gaping hole in the wall. I thought I could harness my seventeen-year-old son's excess energy by employing him and a friend to help with the renovations of the building. One of their jobs was to demolish part of a wall that would be a doorway with steps leading down from my planned studio into a ground level room that would be an art gallery. This, though, wasn't a door-sized hole; it was a wall-sized hole.

Then, I looked to the opposite side of the space where a wall that had enclosed the ladies washroom had already been demolished. The second sledge hammer was perched precariously on one of two smashed porcelain sinks. I'd planned to recycle one of them for the bathroom that would be built upstairs. I dreaded what I might find up there.

Beer bottles, most of them empty, a few containing the disgusting butts of soggy cigarettes, lined the bar. A tipped punch bowl disgorged watermelon rinds and a pool of sticky, red liquid. A garbage bag failed to contain the overflow of empty potato and corn chip bags and pizza boxes. Half-eaten slices of pizza, glued to plates by congealed gobs of mozzarella cheese, looked like petrified specimens. Some beer glasses held remnants of the liquid from the punch bowl while others held the residue of a brown liquid that looked like Coke but smelled like rum.

I noticed an unfamiliar stereo speaker had been left on the platform that had once served as a small stage. Obviously, a party had occurred here on the weekend while I was away. The scene downstairs looked like it had been a demolition party. There was no permanent damage done on the second floor because the space had yet to be renovated from a banquet hall to an apartment for my family. My son used this as his justification for holding a party.

"Ah, Ma, this is such a great space. I wanted my friends to see it."

When questioned on the partially destroyed wall and sinks, he said that he didn't know the sink was to be reused and that the opening in the wall was to be much smaller.

"We thought we were helping," he said.

He was somewhat more contrite about the defacing splats and streams on the front of the building.

"Some kids we didn't know wanted to crash the party. When we wouldn't let them in, they started throwing eggs."

"If you and your friends were inside, why would they bother throwing eggs?" I said.

"Well," and here he hesitated, "they were trying to reach us on the roof." A newly installed skylight, designed to be opened, provided easy access to the flat roof.

Despite my son's subsequent attempts to remove the rivulets of egg from the brick and stucco, the sun had baked them into the textured surface. It was a long time before they were no longer visible. To help compensate for the destroyed sinks and wall, my son's previously paid labor on the renovations became—for a time—voluntary.

CHAPTER TWENTY-SEVEN

My evolving relationship with Suki triggered recollections of the inexplicable bond between mothers and sons. I knew I wasn't the only mother to overlook a son's shortcomings and provide support, whether deserved or not.

"The customer you have dialed is unavailable at the moment."

The flat female voice that greeted me each time I tried to reach Curtis at his cell phone number began to annoy me. Curtis had moved into the bachelor apartment—converted from the art gallery I first built there— three months before,   and now I was beginning to wonder if renting to a twenty-three-year old male had been wise. He had a job working for a roofing company and assured me that he wouldn't be hosting any noisy parties since he'd just moved to Toronto from the small town of Owen Sound and didn't know many people here. I hesitated, thinking of my son's wild and destructive parties.

Curtis's blonde good looks, charming smile and polite manner won out over my initial reluctance to rent to him. Now, not being able to reach him by phone for over two weeks worried me. I hadn't seen him or heard any noises from his apartment in that time. Since I respected my tenant's privacy, I felt uncomfortable as I turned the key and ventured into his apartment.

A laptop computer lay open on the black futon that faced a large flat-screen television. On the floor beside the futon were the television remote control and a glass of water. The bookcases, which came with the apartment, were empty, except for several pieces of mail, only some of which had been opened. Clothes were haphazardly thrown over the arm-chair that I'd loaned to him. The pine harvest table, another loan, held a blue Ikea bowl, remnants of milk and cereal congealed in the bottom. The Honey Nut Cheerios box was still open on the counter beside a blackened banana peel. In the bathroom, an electric razor lay on the sink counter, and white towels, some still with price tags attached, were stacked on the shelf above the toilet. It looked as though Curtis had just stepped out of the apartment and would soon be returning.

I locked the door and went back up the short flight of stairs and down the hallway that led to my studio. Finding the rental application that Curtis had filled out, I was glad I had the foresight to stipulate that his mother be one of his references.

"Hello, is this Barb, Curtis's mother?" I asked.

"Yes," she replied, with hesitation.

I explained that I was Curtis's landlady, described to her the scene in his apartment and said that I was worried about him.

She sighed wearily.

"Curtis came home for a visit two weekends ago and met a buddy who works in the oil sands at Fort McMurray. He convinced Curtis to drive back there with him at the end of the weekend. I suppose he owes you money. How much?"

Within a few days, a bank draft arrived from Barb, a friend had come to collect Curtis's laptop computer, television and clothing, and I was once again faced with the difficult task of finding a new tenant. From *then on, I made it a policy to not only get the phone number of prospective young tenants' mothers but to also phone and talk to them.*

Friday, February 21, 1992

What to say to asshole's mother? I find your support of John inappropriate and hurtful. If you want to help him live with his selfish values then I do not want to talk to you. Your support of him reinforces his warped way of thinking that what he did was right. It is not right and it will never be right.

Chapter Twenty-Eight

I was invited to a cremation by Made. He was particularly friendly and talkative because he wanted to practice his English. The ceremony was for his aunt. The day before the ceremony he came to apologize—he couldn't transport me to the cremation ceremony himself because as a member of the family he had duties to perform. Suki just happened to be visiting at that time (perhaps this wasn't a coincidence), so it was arranged that Suki would take me to the cremation. We planned to combine it with a snorkeling expedition to the wreck as it was close to the location for the cremation. The following excerpt is from the Frommer's guide to Bali and Lombok. It explains the ceremony, and it was a useful source of information. I think Suki thought his role was strictly to provide transportation; he wasn't a tour guide.

Ashes to Ashes, Dust to Dust: Cremation

Cremation is the most important ceremony in the Balinese life cycle, as it is said to release the soul. It is a time for celebration, not sorrow, and thus is wonderfully colorful. People will begin saving for their cremation in middle age. The average family spends about RP 15 million on the ceremony, about a year's wages, while wealthy families have been known to lavish hundreds of millions of rupiahs. If there is not enough money saved, families may have to wait years, sometimes more than a decade, before they can hold a cremation. In this case, bodies are buried and then exhumed after enough money has been saved and collected from the community for the cremation. The cremation is always on an auspicious day chosen by the priest from the local or nearby village, according to the Balinese calendar and the movement of the moon.

A large bamboo tower, its size and shape dictated by the caste of the dead person, is built for the cremation. A wooden life size bull (for men) or cow (for women) is sometimes carved. On the morning of the cremation, the family of the deceased entertains friends and relatives and then the body is placed inside the bamboo tower. The village *kul-kul* (wooden gong) is struck and the construction is carried in noisy procession to the cremation ground by the *banjar* (village community members).

Suki and I joined a long stream of people on foot, on motorcycles and in a few cars, behind the ceremonial procession to the ocean. The cremation briar was far ahead followed by people from all the surrounding villages. Next in the procession was the gamelan band providing a rhythmic processional beat. The end of the parade was comprised of a straggling group of Westerners. Some, including me, were wearing the proper attire, sarong and sash, but others were dressed in tank tops and shorts. I felt embarrassed by their inappropriate dress.

We approached a point in the road that was under water. No

bridge. The water simply flowed over the road on its way to the ocean. All of the local people forded the water without stopping. They were all wearing flip-flops. I'd made the wrong choice of footwear, leather sandals that would take days to dry if I used them as wading shoes. To my right was a white couple, the husband chivalrously ferrying his wife across the river on his back. Suki looked at the comically teetering couple but didn't make the same offer. Although taller and of a more muscular build than the average Balinese male, he wasn't prepared to bear my substantial weight. Off came my sandals and in I went in my bare feet.

We arrived at a beach covered with colorful fishing boats. The procession had stopped under a huge banyan tree. Now I could see what appeared to be not one but two briars. The largest one contained an impressive black bull sculpture constructed like one of the *ogoh-ogoh* sculptures. Beside it was a much smaller, less elaborate one. There were to be two cremations, for a man and a woman.

About fifty large offering baskets containing fruit, rice, eggs and flowers covered a platform to one side. One basket held bamboo sticks topped by pink and white puffed rice cakes. Some were decorated with bright pink icing. Right beside me on a stick that was leaning against the platform was a very tiny barbequed pig. Not much of a meal there.

Three gaunt older women, with sharply defined cheekbones, fussed over the offerings. They rearranged them on the platform and opened and closed plastic bags to check the contents. Their fussing over the food reminded me of the receptions given at my church after funerals. Often, ladies in the congregation were asked to provide refreshments. It seemed that in both Bali and Canada, the lavishness of the spread reflected the status of the deceased.

The *banjar* carried the briars three times around the immense tree. Topped by Western umbrellas, the briars passed under low branches that snagged the higher of the two umbrellas—the one on the man's briar—on each circuit. It emerged dangling and damaged.

The men removed a lid from the bull sculpture's body and proceeded to fill the cavity with objects, including a brand new mattress still wrapped in plastic and an umbrella. They placed a filing cabinet made from particle board on the platform with the bull, the keys still dangling from one of the drawer locks.

The woman's briar was lower and mostly obscured from my sight; I couldn't see what was placed on it. There were two whooshes and the onlookers fell back. The cremation briars had been ignited. The flames were intense and every once in a while additional whooshes kept the briars burning violently. I couldn't understand how they could burn so fiercely until I noticed a metal pipe shoved under the larger briar. About ten feet away, a man was holding the pipe at a juncture where it changed from a metal pipe to a plastic hose. The hose was obviously connected to a source of fuel.

The eyes of possibly three hundred people were riveted on the blazing briars. It was difficult to estimate the number because of the way the people were packed in around the tree and along the beach. All of them stayed for the hour it took to reduce the briars to twisted and charred piles of metal rods and wire. Nearly everyone stood during the cremation. The only exception was a group of young men, crouched on their haunches near the water, smoking and talking. The ceremony ended when two priests started whisking purification water at the crowd as they exited past the offerings platform.

Suki had waited for me with my snorkeling equipment bag at the far edge of the crowd. He was alone, which was unusual, since most of the other young men had congregated in groups. It crossed my mind that either he didn't know many of these people or was embarrassed to be seen with me.

As we walked back to his motorcycle, Suki suggested we postpone our snorkeling as we had already spent two hours at the cremation. I realized when we got back to Double One Villas that we couldn't have gone snorkeling anyway; I'd forgotten to take my bathing suit.

In an email home to my children, I suggested they start saving for my cremation on a beach in Bali.

January 22, 1993

My flower images as flowers for my funeral placed on the walls around the room.

Installation — Beauty in the Face of Pain.

Flower drawings surrounding a coffin — death of a marriage — death of a salesman — Willy Loman — the artist as an anti-Willy Loman — easier having a 9-5 job to structure one's life and not have to fight with self-discipline.

Idea — Get flower arrangements from funeral home — Death in the face of beauty — Beauty in the face of death.

Continue blue flowers as a diptych.

Pills and booze.

CHAPTER TWENTY-NINE

During my stay in Bali, I noticed glass and plastic bottles containing a light-colored liquid displayed on outdoor shelves at many of the variety stores at the edge of the road. There were no labels on the bottles, they were all different sizes and didn't look new. I'd assumed that they were bottles of *arak*, the Balinese version of moonshine.

Finally, I saw a hand-lettered sign written in English and discovered the mystery liquid was petrol for the motorcycles. The few gas stations were found only in the largest towns, so these handy roadside stalls provided fuel for the thousands of motorcycles. I was glad I hadn't followed through on my idea of purchasing one of these bottles to sample the local hooch. The consequences would have been dire. Suki would have lost his sole source of income, and my whim of being cremated on a Balinese beach would become a reality.

The inevitable happened—Suki had acquired another woman. He

told me he was driving a German woman from her rented villa to an internet place every day. I was relieved not to be Suki's only customer. Although he seemed to be spending long periods of time with her, it didn't stop him from hanging around asking when he could transport me again to snorkel at the cove with the Japanese wreck.

July 10, 1993

Missing Stephen more all the time. Agonize over calling or writing him. Went to singles dance and danced with lots of people, but there was no spark except for one guy who physically attracted me, but we didn't seem to have many interests in common — Jerry — coffee man.

Tall man — intelligent — collected botanical drawings — Dan.

Short guy — doctor who bragged about money — obnoxious in wanting my phone number.

Nerdy guy — landscape architect.

Chinese young guy.

Don was there — he seems the professional smooth guy, but he's not great looking.

Makes me despair of ever finding a soul mate. Depressing.

When Suki persuaded me that the conditions for snorkeling were ideal, we went again. We climbed on his motorcycle—without helmets—zoomed up the hills, around the bends, through the river crossing the road, scaring the roosters off the roadway and beeping wildly as we passed other motorcycles. I was no longer as scared being a passenger and even started to look at the mountainous coastal landscape.

The current was a little stronger that day. Knowing now that Suki wasn't a strong swimmer, I had visions of me rescuing him from the grip of the current, not the other way around. When he signaled that he had a cramp in his leg and was going back to shore, I relaxed, knowing that my life-saving skills were not to be tested.

It seemed I might become the benefactor for Suki's whole extended family. I discovered that a boy about twelve years old, trying to sell me a toy replica of the fishing boats was his nephew. Suki had already sold me two of these boats, but his nephew persisted in his sales pitch.

"You not have big boat," he said.

"There isn't enough room in my suitcase for two little boats *and* a big one," I responded.

I felt justified buying the two boats from Suki when I discovered him on the beach whittling a boat hull from a stick. He had made the boats himself and had taken them back to his home to paint the names of my grandchildren on each one.

Many members of his family were creative. He showed me what he called a calendar, hoping I would buy it.

"This made by uncle," Suki said as he opened up the art object.

It was similar in structure to a venetian blind. The slats were made of palm leaves except the top and bottom ones, which were bamboo. Ordinary white kitchen string held the slats together and made possible their collapse into a compact bundle. Very delicate, embossed lines illustrated a story about the god Rama, and the back of each slat was etched with the words of the story in fractured English. Knowing that I was an artist, Suki thought I would appreciate the artistry of the illustrations. The regular price was three hundred and fifty thousand rupiah—about thirty-five American dollars. He had discussed the price with the uncle's business manager, who was Suki's aunt and the artist's wife.

"I ask aunt give special price. For Canadian mother."

How could I refuse such a personal sales pitch?

Some days at Double One Villas, there would be two or three other guests who stayed only one night. Lily had left to spend a few days in Kuta before flying home to Australia where she was a psychologist specializing in working with special needs children.

On my seventh day there, Suki announced that three new guests had arrived.

"Old women, like you," he said.

He didn't realize he had insulted me. To him, I was an old woman, with adult children and grandchildren. My worst fears about turning sixty had been confirmed. To the rest of the world, or at least to a young man in Bali, I was an old woman.

I was curious to meet these other "old" ladies, a meeting that occurred that evening at dinner. Dede, Sue and Janet were three very jolly women from Brisbane, Australia. Janet had been coming to Bali for ten years, but this was the first visit for her friends. Like Lily, Janet had become a benefactor for some of the local people. Both of them had arranged for children to be sponsored, specifically to pay for their education, by friends and relatives back home in Australia. Janet had brought clothing and school supplies for her Balinese friends, in particular for the staff and their families at Double One Villas.

They headed out for a tour of local orphanages. Her friends reported back that Janet had delivered five watermelons as a gift to one of the orphanages and bought fresh vegetables for their driver's family. They had played a game of Frisbee with the children and left the Frisbee behind as a souvenir of their visit.

Sue was a tough old bird, smoked constantly, had the husky voice that goes with it and had a wicked sense of humor. She soon addressed me as "darling" and was quick to confide details of her life and the lives of her companions. Dede, nicknamed to distinguish her from the other Janet with the same name, was a cool, reserved, auburn-haired woman. It wasn't a surprise to find out she was a retired assistant school principal. The other Janet, called *Ebu Janet* because she had assumed the role of a generous mother, was a rather ample woman, quick to offer all sorts of advice and information about Bali and the charitable agencies that she belonged to in Bali. Three years ago, *Ebu Janet* and Lily had met in Amed. They had both come to a resort called Dancing Dragon for a retreat that offered courses in feng shui. From Lily, I'd heard the sad saga of the fate of Dancing Dragon and from *Ebu Janet*, I heard Lily's story. It seems that older Australian women are intrepid storytellers, especially if those stories are about other older Australian women.

CHAPTER THIRTY

The Story of Dancing Dragon Cottages
As Told by Lily and Janet

Keep in mind that the truth is sometimes stretched by storytellers and that the person listening sometimes has a bad memory.

Susan Dover, an internationally recognized author and expert in feng shui, often came to Bali. In Amed, she met a Balinese man who I will call Chi (certain names have been changed). In Bali, a man can have more than one wife at a time, and so Susan became Chi's second wife. By Balinese law, only citizens can buy and own land, so with Chi's right to own land and Susan's money, they purchased an oceanfront lot near Amed and built a resort. It was designed by Susan as a feng shui resort, and feng shui elements were the guiding principle for the harmonious design and placement of the cottages, pool and open dining area. Susan offered feng shui and space clearing seminars, and it was at one of these that Lily and Janet met.

The Susan/Chi union was not a harmonious one. Susan met a fellow Australian, divorced Chi and married David. David was the former manager of a five-star hotel in Australia, and he tried to apply Western standards to upgrade Dancing Dragon. He instituted payment by credit card, installed an ATM machine and a cappuccino machine. As Lily told the story, he had all the staff come for a day's training on the machine, paid them nothing for attending and didn't even provide meals. Lily said he lacked any sensitivity to the needs and character of the Balinese staff. She received calls from some of them, terrified that they would lose their jobs if they didn't live up to David's outrageously high standards. David also forbade the fishermen from walking through the resort to gain access to their boats on the beach in front of the resort.

Chi, still the official land owner, turned against Susan and new husband David and froze the joint bank account used to run Dancing Dragon. Many of the staff were his disgruntled relatives.

The story, now told by Janet, got even more complex and interesting. By now, Lily had also met a Balinese man (note the pattern developing) named Mono, who worked as a driver for Dancing Dragon. Lily was a childless widow and threw herself into keeping the resort afloat. By this time, Susan and David had exited to Susan's villa somewhere else in Bali. Lily talked Chi into keeping Dancing Dragon running. She agreed to pay the staff's wages for six months, hoping that this would buy enough time for the resort to revert back to peace and profitability. Chi was happy to have his relatives employed, and Lily was happy to have Mono employed.

Susan, however, wanted to recoup some of her expenditures on the buildings and put the business up for sale. No buyer stepped forward to buy a floundering business without the security of owning the land too. Chi pulled the plug on the whole thing. Susan emptied the buildings of all the furniture and fixtures and sold them. The resort stood empty, neglected and derelict.

To make the story even more convoluted, Chi also owned the hotel two lots over, Double One Villas. With the demise of Dancing Dragon, Lily stayed at Double One, and Mono and his brother became the standby drivers. As a concession to Lily's paying six months of staff wages at the former Dancing Dragon, Chi agreed to give her a preferential lodging rate and free dinners, for her alone, in the dining room. While she was telling me this long and involved story, although some of the story came from Janet, she was fuming that Chi had reneged on this agreement. He was now an absentee owner and a member of parliament (hence the discretion of not revealing his real name), so Lily had no one to complain to except me and the staff. I overheard her several times refusing to sign her dinner bill.

By now (this is where Janet takes over the story again), Lily had become Mono's second wife and he lived with her at Double One Villas when she was in Bali. He would move back in with his first Balinese wife and three children when Lily returned to Australia to work. According to Janet, Lily had bought Mono and his first wife a house and also bought a rice farm for Mono's parents. With Mono's name and her money, they had bought a vacant lot between Dancing Dragon and Double One Villas and were also building a villa on land in Sanur.

As Janet joked to me, "You didn't know you had stumbled on the equivalent of Peyton Place in the sleepy little village of Amed!"

Sue also had stories to tell involving Australian women and Balinese men. Her story involved a friend of Janet's from Brisbane. This friend had obviously heard of Susan and Lily's experiences with Balinese men. She wanted to come to Bali, and Janet helped her to book accommodation at Double One Villas and arranged for a driver to pick her up at the airport. As soon as she arrived, according to Sue, she demanded the staff send a man to her room. She wasn't at all attractive, of a more mature age—as am I and all of the Western women in these stories—and had a demanding and prickly personality. None of the staff had any interest at all in being "the man." One of them fetched a local fisherman, and he was the lucky, or unlucky, depending on how you look at it, recipient of the woman's ardor.

Sue laughed her husky, raucous laugh and snorted, "And she didn't even pay him!"

At this point in the conversation, Janet teased her friends to tell me about their airport purchases. With much laughter and not much embarrassment, Sue revealed that she and Dede had bought condoms at the Bali airport.

"The ones made in Australia are too big for Balinese men," she said.

Apparently, Bali is to some Australian women what Thailand is to some Australian men. Sue asked if I'd ever heard of the "Thai Venetian Blind Tan" and slyly winked as she suggested that there was a Balinese version of the Venetian Blind Tan.

"Lorna, you've got enough time left to get your own Balinese husband."

The account of the Australian women helped to explain some of the puzzling situations I'd found myself in since my arrival in Bali, starting with the offer of Made, my first driver, to transport me to Kuta. I googled "Kuta Bali sex" on my netbook and came up with many references to Kuta Cowboys including a documentary called "Cowboys in Paradise," which explored Bali's reputation as the world's leading destination for female sex tourists. Up to then, I was oblivious to the perception of many of the people I met that I'd traveled to Bali to find a boy toy.

Maybe that explained why Suki asked to use my shower after our first snorkel excursion. I said he should go ahead, and he gave me a funny look when I said I planned to have a swim in the pool and would shower later. Perhaps the mysterious small packet, which he had asked me to put in my bag on our wet ride back from Amlapura, was a package of condoms. It was the right size and shape, and he had purchased it at what looked like a drug store. Were these clues, which I had obviously not picked up, that he was offering more than just rides on his motorcycle?

Could it also explain the invitation to share a drink with the staff on *Nyepi* only to discover that I was the only woman in a group of five men? Was I expected to make a choice among them of a *special friend* like some of my fellow mature Western women? In the eyes of Suki and these other young men, I was a source of potential income and was a disappointment to them when I was too naïve to read the clues.

Janet, Dede and Sue stayed in Amed for only three nights. I always wondered if they had had any opportunity to use their airport purchases.

I discovered as I read the menu at Wawa Wewe II, the hotel next door, that Dancing Dragon Cottages lived on in name, if not in fact. Wawa Wewe II had either bought or been given the fancy, heavy books that were designed to hold menu pages. A wooden plaque glued to the sturdy front cover was carved with the name "Dancing Dragon Restaurant." The economic benefits of recycling were not lost on the Balinese.

CHAPTER THIRTY-ONE

The night before the Australian women were to leave Amed, I arrived for a late dinner at the beachside dining area. Although it was only seven in the evening, and they were supposed to serve dinner until nine o'clock, the two staff members advised me that I had to eat dinner in the reception area dining space at the top of the hill beside the road. I was a little put out as I liked to eat beside the water with only the sound of the waves, crickets, frogs and roosters. Besides, it was an arduous climb up multiple flights of tall steps.

There seemed to be a lot of people in the reception area, their voices raised in confusion and fear. *Ebu* Janet appeared to have assumed a leadership role, a fitting one given her physical heft.

"Haven't you heard the news?" she said.

"What news?" I asked bluntly. I get cranky when I'm hungry.

The hotel had no radio, television or newspapers. I purposely didn't check the news on the internet since I didn't want to know what was going on in the world.

"We've got to evacuate our rooms," she said. "My daughter called from Australia. There's been a massive earthquake. Bali will be hit by a huge tsunami at eight o'clock. Go back to your room. Get your passport and come back here."

In the background hubbub, I heard the words, "Earthquake, six point seven on the Richter scale; we've got to leave," and decided it was prudent to do as she said until I could find out more.

Once I reached my room, I thought that if what she said was true, I should pack a small bag with essentials in addition to my passport. I grabbed my blood pressure pills from the bathroom sink and a fabric bag that already contained a miniature drugstore that included Tylenol, diarrhea medicine, Gravol and antibiotics. I hesitated at the bottle of Pepto Bismol, a mouthful of which I took every morning as a guard against stomach and bowel upsets. I decided against taking it because of its large size. I threw in my notebooks, camera, camera charger, netbook computer and its power cord, my small flashlight, a pair of panties (hoping that they were clean ones), a t-shirt (that I knew for certain was dirty), a rain jacket, sweater, traveling alarm clock, a folding paper calendar that had photographs of my grandson as part of its design, my money belt and purse. In my haste, I almost forgot what I'd come for, my passport. I went back up the hill with my bulging blue nylon bag.

The words had changed. Now it was, "Earthquake in Japan, forty meter high tsunami hitting Bali at eight o'clock, start walking higher up the mountain."

Tsunami! I went back down the hill to my room to get my fluorescent orange rain cape and umbrella. The umbrella would be useful for either deflecting falling debris from an earthquake or as protection from water in the event of a tsunami. The cape could be used as a ground sheet for sleeping, could be rigged up to act as a miniature shelter and would be easily spotted from the air by a rescuing helicopter. I was prepared for anything.

Back up the hill I went. It was getting crowded in the reception area. The staff looked confused and were quiet. Two Canadian couples, guests who had arrived that day, had just come back from having dinner at a neighboring hotel. They looked puzzled, having only just heard the conflicting news. All three Australians were on their cell phones, yelling loudly into them to their relatives in Australia.

Having been denied my dinner in the lower dining room, I thought that it would be impossible to get a meal in the midst of this chaos. Sue had lost contact with Australia on her cell, and she came over to share more of the catastrophic news. I said I was hungry and she offered me her dinner and what was left of Dede's sitting unattended at a table nearby. She wondered how I could remain so calm, cool and collected.

"How can you eat at a time like this?" she asked.

I responded pragmatically. "If I'm going to die, I might as well have a full stomach." She didn't laugh.

Two strangers, guests at the hotel beside us, Wawa Wewe II, were sitting at a table trying to find information on their laptop computer. Incongruously, a young European couple with a boy of about five were casually having dinner, not understanding or caring what was going on because they didn't speak either Balinese or English.

I leaned in over the shoulder of one of the men on the laptop trying to read what was on the screen. Since my head was almost touching his, I figured I should introduce myself.

"Hi, I'm Lorna from Toronto, Canada."

"I'm Tom from Niagara-on-the-Lake and this is John, from Fort Erie."

"Canadians, eh?" I said.

Perhaps in their late forties, they were traveling Bali on motorcycles. The term "good old boys" struck me as the way to describe them. John kept using the phrase "Right on." They had wandered up the hill from Wawa Wewe II to use the WIFI at our hotel. They were now enmeshed in the impending crisis and hoopla generated by the Australian women.

Tom and John had spent the previous night in Kuta, the main tourist destination and party town in Bali. At three in the morning, they were jarred from their sleep by the shaking sensation of an earthquake.

"We were a little wasted. Figured it wasn't worth getting out of bed," Tom said.

Eko was standing nearby. "I feel shake, too," he said. "Small, not big."

I, however, had slept through it.

Tom finally found a website that confirmed an earthquake had indeed occurred early in the morning. The site reported that it was of six point eight intensity, had occurred in the Bali Sea but was so deep below the surface of the ocean that there had been no danger at all of a tsunami occurring.

Then Tom found another website reporting that a major earthquake had occurred late in the day off the coast of Northern Japan, and it told of the devastation from a huge tsunami that had hit part of the Japanese coast. Jerky videos showed the destruction as the tsunami hit a coastal city. The huge wall of water carried large, capsized boats from the harbor and propelled them crazily up a river, grabbing cars, trucks and buildings and smashing them against a bridge.

At least two earthquakes had occurred on the same day, the non-destructive one close by in the Bali Sea and the horrendously damaging one in Japan. There was a possibility of the tsunami generated in Japan reaching islands in Indonesia to the north of Bali. There was more risk of it reaching the west coasts of Canada and the United States than there was of it reaching Bali.

Janet, the disaster instigator, miffed at the composure of the Canadians in the reception area, thrust a cell phone in my face to have me listen to the exhortations of an Australian friend of hers living in Kuta.

"Your side of the island is going to be hit by the tsunami. You need to get to higher ground," she yelled.

I thanked her for her advice and handed the phone back to Janet, who was still fuming at our calm demeanor.

At this point, I powered up my netbook to try, in tandem with Tom on his laptop, to get accurate information from the internet. The internet may be the ultimate source for up-to-date information, but in this case, the sheer number of websites to open slowed both of us down in our quest for reliable information.

The estimated time for Armageddon of eight o'clock came and went. It might prove to be a long night so John retrieved a bottle of vodka from his hotel room next door. With as little room as they had for storage on their motorcycles, they still managed to make room for a bottle of vodka. John also brought back the power cord for the laptop because the battery had run out.

John tried to buy a bag of ice from Eko who was totally uncomprehending, or pretended to be.

"No ice?" he said. "There must be someplace around here where we can buy a bag of ice."

He had no idea of the limited resources on a dark, rainy Friday night in a simple fishing village in Bali.

"John, I haven't seen many Seven Eleven stores nearby," I said.

"Right on," he replied.

He worked out an arrangement with Eko that they would be supplied with ice if they bought the mix from the hotel. They generously offered me a vodka and tonic with lime. I wouldn't only die with a full stomach; I would also have a drunken smile on my face.

The Australian women, who would have normally enjoyed a drink, were still too overwrought to share in the liquid refreshments. A young British woman and her French boyfriend wandered up the hill from the deserted Wawa Wewe II, wondering what all the commotion at Double One Villas was about. They brought their own libations, a large water bottle filled with *arak*. The disaster party had begun!

Finding that the internet wasn't very useful as a source of information—it provided too much information, some of it contradictory— I tried SKYPING my children in Canada and a friend in Florida. I'd forgotten that Alison, my son-in-law Gareth and grandson Griffin weren't in Canada but in Cuba. Andrew didn't have SKYPE turned on and I left a voice message for my friend when he didn't answer the SKYPE call.

I sent email messages to all of them saying that it seemed we were in no immediate danger. This was the message a staff member brought to all of us congregated in the reception area. The Indonesian government had broadcast the information on television. The staff member had watched it at his home in the village.

Janet, Dede and Sue settled down on hearing the news that the end was not imminent. Janet was the owner of a New Age crystal shop in Brisbane.

"I've got nine clairvoyants working for my shop. I've a mind to fire the lot of them when I get home. Not one of them divined this bloody tsunami," she said.

The Australian women occupied the two oceanside bungalows. They were still too upset to go back there to sleep, and so they lugged their pillows up the hill to bunk down in the reception area for the night.

"My villa's half-way up the hill," I told them. "Much higher than even a monster tsunami could reach. More comfortable than sleeping here. Besides, I need to be up early for a tour."

Even though my bungalow was located a fair distance away from the reception area, I could hear the party continuing well into the early hours of the morning. Janet confirmed the next day that, after initially protesting to the partygoers that they were occupying her sleeping space, she, Dede and Sue had joined the party. When the party finally broke up, the Australians returned to sleep in their bungalows, and the Wawa Weweers stumbled down the steep driveway to their hotel.

As a postscript to the evening's festivities, Janet told me the story of her retreat up the hill to the reception area. She had been sleeping when the staff came to her door to tell her to leave her bungalow. Janet was hefty and not very lithe on her feet. Two of the relatively petite Balinese men pulled each of her hands from the front. The third was employed to push her broad behind up the steep and wet stone steps. Without warning, she lost her footing in one of the dark intervals where there were no lights. She crashed to the ground taking all three of the Balinese men with her. She was on the bottom, and they were in a heap on top of her.

"Lucky for those blokes I'm well-padded," she said with a good humored laugh.

CHAPTER THIRTY-TWO

The next day, I managed to wake up early despite the previous night's excitement. I'd become complacent about staying in one place and not seeing more of Bali. Suki asked almost every day about taking a car tour, and I finally agreed. The driver was his friend Nyoman, a man with slightly popping eyes and a broad Cheshire cat smile that revealed perfectly straight teeth. Between the ages of fifteen and seventeen, the Balinese have the points on their incisor teeth filed flat in a special ceremony. The purpose of the ceremony is to remove impurity by eliminating or reducing the six deadly sins: lust, greed, anger, drunkenness, confusion and jealously that are symbolized by the upper canine teeth.

"Nyoman, what's your second name?" I needed something to distinguish him from all the other Nyomans I was meeting.

The word he mumbled sounded to me like "Pasta."

"Ah, your parents wanted you to work with food," I said.

Suki noticed his friend's confusion caused by my interpretation of his name.

"Name mean dance," Suki said.

I turned to Nyoman. "So you're a dancer."

"Not dancer, driver. More money for family," he replied.

Although Nyoman called himself a driver, he didn't own a car. He arrived driving a rental car on the appointed day and time. Suki was to go along as my guide. They were both waiting for me on the stairs next to my bungalow when I came up from having breakfast.

The weather was similar to what it was almost every morning, overcast, but with occasional patches of blue sky. I am not a sun worshipper. If I don't wear sunscreen, I get burnt, which results in either peeling skin or the appearance of more freckles eventually merging into a brown mottled mess.

We headed north along the coastal road passing through many small villages. Bypass roads don't exist in Bali, so even a trip of a short distance, involves traveling over narrow, potholed and congested roads through each village. On this particular trip, two rather nasty potholes in the center of the road were marked by plastic chairs. Driving through two of the larger villages, I noticed produce markets. In one town, stalls were sheltered by a tin roof. In the other village, the food vendors had spread their fruit and vegetables out on cloths or tarps on the ground. I saw more of the countryside and the villages from the car than I had from the back of a motorcycle. On the motorcycle, I was distracted by thoughts of horrible accidents.

I requested one special stop. My Frommer's guide book recommended visiting a women's co-operative weaving workshop called Surya Indigo that used the ancient tradition of bebali weaving on once abandoned cagcag looms. The weaving workshop was also unique in its use of traditional dyes derived from natural sources. Five women operated the looms on a roofed platform that offered better working conditions than the textile workshop I'd visited in Sideman.

The manager, Nyoman Sarmika, took me on a tour, showing me the trees, plants and spices that were used in the dyeing process. Only five colors of natural dyes were used in their weaving. Indigo was extracted from the leaves of a bush, and turmeric root produced a rich orange color. Yellow was made from the bark of the jackfruit tree and red was produced from the roots of the morinda plant. He showed me hanks of cotton thread dyed in these colors hanging on a line to dry. Some of their rarer and most exquisite textiles were woven from silk threads.

"Our textiles are thought to have magical powers," Nyoman said. "They have been used for many years to protect against evil spirits." The piece of fabric he held in his hands shimmered in the intense sunlight, its silky chameleon skin changing color—gold, silver, copper—as the angle of the light changed.

"I tried dyeing cloth with indigo many years ago," I told Nyoman. "The color washed out. Someone told me I needed to use urine to make it colorfast."

"Come and learn dyeing here," Nyoman said. "It is my dream that women like you from many countries can come here to work with our women. Money from project like this will help to keep our workshop going."

"I'd like to do that," I replied.

I liked the idea of being part of the creative energy of this project and its goal of keeping alive a traditional Balinese art practice.

The long process of dyeing and weaving meant that the output of the workshop was limited. The store attached to the workshop had only a few lengths of fabric for sale because they had sold most of their stock.

Does the magic of bebali cloth work? I bought the delicately-hued silk shawl that Nyoman showed me, as a gift for my daughter Alison. At the time she and her husband were trying, unsuccessfully, for a second child.

"This is for the baby's christening," I said as I gave it to her. "In Bali, this fabric has special powers."

She looked at me doubtfully.

Galen, my third grandchild, was born within a year.

For our second stop, we left the coastal road at the village of Les and drove up a winding road into the mountains. The attraction at the end of the road was, at a height of ninety-eight feet, one of the highest waterfalls in Bali. Nyoman chose to stay with the car. He had already experienced the trek up the mountain to the site of the water-fall. Suki set out at a furious pace, and I noticed he had exchanged the flip-flops he always wore for a pair of runners. I struggled to keep up with him, and he didn't look back to see how I was doing.

On the way up the steep path, we passed two farms, although farm is much too grand a word to use. One of the farms consisted of two tiny huts, a small garden, two cows, a few chickens and, of course, some roosters. We met a farmer carrying two baskets of cow manure on a shoulder yoke. That might have been the extent of his farm's output—natural fertilizer to sell to other farmers.

Effortlessly, Suki climbed the path to the waterfall. I was starting to have new thoughts about not surviving my Bali trip. Rather than meeting my demise while on the back of a motorcycle or being swept away in a fast current while snorkeling alone, it was possible I was go-ing to suffer a heart attack on the side of a mountain.

Just when I was about to yell ahead to Suki that I needed a rest break, I could hear the sound of the waterfall. We rounded a curve in the trail and there it was in all its sparkling beauty. Trees and foliage partially obscured our view. Suki veered off the path to the edge of the river flowing from the base of the falls, took off his shoes and waded in to cross the river for a better view. I followed him, took one look at the sharp stones in the river and decided to leave my shoes on. Expensive leather sandals were never designed as wading shoes. The choice was to ruin the soles of my feet or ruin the shoes. Feet can't be replaced; shoes can. I rolled up my pant legs and waded into the river.

The view from the other side of the river was better, but Suki de-cided, without consultation, that we needed to go back in the water and wade closer to the base of the falls. I looked down at my poor soggy shoes, the leather already beginning to stretch out of shape, and decided to take them off. It was a bad decision. The rocks in the river were sharp and slippery, and I teetered this way and that looking for smoother rocks to step onto. My feet were slipping, and I worried I might turn an ankle so I tried grasping at roots and bushes at the river's edge to help keep steady and upright.

I couldn't stand the pain from the sharp stones on my soft bare soles, so I swallowed my pride and yelled ahead to Suki to come back and help me. I grasped the hand he reluctantly held out. Of all the people in Bali who wanted to earn money as guides, why did I have to get someone who was such a failure at this job? Maybe his skills were better developed in his other income-producing occupation. He let go of my hand as soon as he possibly could, and we stood in the cold river water silently admiring the waterfall. It was a narrow waterfall but so high and overhung by foliage that we could barely see the source of the plunging water.

Wading out of the water, I saw that if we had stayed on the footpath, we would have eventually reached this spot without having to sacrifice the soles of my feet and a nearly new pair of shoes. It was then that I realized this was Suki's first visit to the waterfall and he didn't know where the path ended.

Chapter Thirty-Three

Back in the car, I suggested to Nyoman that we stop someplace for lunch, and it would be my treat. Why is it that drivers and/or guides take their customers to overpriced tourist traps with bad buffets? This one was at a hotel in Lovina, a town I'd been contemplating as my next destination because of its reputation as a good snorkeling spot. I wasn't impressed with either the town or the look of the ocean, murky and rough, and I abandoned my plan to move there from Amed. As my escort, Suki ate with me, but Nyoman disappeared into the kitchen where the food was probably better.

Our final stop of the day was at a village called Banjar where there was an *Air Panas*. In Balinese, *Air* means water (a confusing translation) and *Panas* means hot. We visited the hot springs bathing pools, and this time it was Nyoman who joined me in the pool while Suki watched from the sidelines. Water spouts shaped like dragon's mouths directed the hot water from an underground spring into two pools, one below the other. I let the hot, sulfurous water tumble from one of the dragon's mouths onto my neck and shoulders. It had the same effect as hot water in a Jacuzzi; the pulsing heat of the water massaging my sore muscles. I let the water spill onto my head, keeping my eyes closed as the water streamed down my face.

The drumming of the water on my head drowned out the sound of a family nearby with two young children who were splashing and playing in the pool. The little girl and boy were in their underwear, the mother was in a t-shirt and shorts, and the father was also wearing shorts. Their appearance was in stark contrast to another group sharing the smaller upper pool. Three European women and a teenage girl were all wearing bikinis that barely covered their fat bodies.

I moved down into the larger lower pool and lay floating on my back letting the warm water support my body and relaxing all my muscles. A light rain started falling. The rain drops seemed to bounce and created dimples when they hit the surface of the hot mineral water. The cold raindrops cooled the air above the pool, creating a steaming mist. Although there were a few other people in the pool, I felt as though I was floating through a solitary dreamscape.

The rain became torrential on our drive back to Amed. The road was flooded in low places with rivers of water. I was worried that the car would stall while driving through these wide swaths of flowing water.

"Will we make it through all this water?" I asked.

"This small rain," Nyoman responded. "In December much water on road. Have to sleep in car with many cars and trucks. Three days."

"If that happens, I claim the back seat as my bed," I said.

Suki joined in on the contingency planning. "I sleep in back," he said, gesturing to the cargo area.

I was a captive audience in the car, and Nyoman launched into a sales pitch.

"You like Bali?" he said.

"Yes, I do. It's beautiful," I responded.

"You buy land here. Suki buy for you. You pay. Build villa. Rent when not here. Free place to stay with family on holiday. Not *have* to marry Suki. Pay five to seven percent for Suki's name on deed."

"Too far to travel and too much money for any of that to happen," I replied.

I could see why this arrangement would appeal to Australian women like Lily who had only a three-and-a-half-hour flight to Bali. I experienced the same uncomfortable feeling with this offer of an opportunity to own a piece of paradise as I had when subjected to the bullying tactics of a time-share salesman in Mexico. Fortunately, Nyoman wasn't as aggressive as the Mexican salesman. He dropped his pitch when I explained how long it took to fly from Toronto to Bali. This wasn't the last time I would be the target of this particular sales offer in Bali.

Arriving home to Double One Villas at six-thirty in the evening, we learned that it had poured rain all day there. Our timing for a tour of the north part of the island had been perfect.

Chapter Thirty-Four

A rainy afternoon was a good time to sit on my porch and write. I designated my porch, with its panoramic view of the hillside garden, my "office." Writing wasn't restricted to my office. I took my notebook everywhere. I wrote while eating. I wrote while walking along the beach. I wrote in bed. Not only was I writing this story, but I was also writing down the names of staff and bits of Balinese phrases that they were trying to teach me. I wrote down the names of other hotels and villages that people told me I should be visiting. I used my notebook to try to figure out the time in Canada by drawing a clock face. Even with that visual aid, I kept getting it wrong. I was out by one whole day in a scheduled SKYPE call to Alison. I used my notebook to figure out how much money I owed the hotel when I paid every five or six days. At one point, I was mildly annoyed when there were other guests because I felt obliged to talk to them when we were having breakfast and it interfered with my writing.

I was gradually coming to know myself better. I realized that I'd always had a running commentary going on in my head. My self-talk didn't always have positive outcomes. I often mulled over minute details of my relationships with men. This sometimes resulted in making assumptions in my head that would have been better communicated to the person involved. I talked myself into believing this or that about a person whether this opinion was valid or not. Since I worked mainly alone as an artist, I had lots of time and opportunity to obsess and pass judgment. My self-talk tended to be negative.

March 28, 1993

Theme of death & mortality at church.
Last week—what gives life meaning? Male/female unit is strong for me.

Ask Merv—am I a negative person? Is introversion and questioning life's meaningfulness a crime? Did I make John's life unhappy or did he make his own life unhappy? It must have been me if things are so much better now with a different person.

I was learning on this trip that by writing out my thoughts, I released them to the page, and they became less obsessive. Writing became a form of therapy and a cathartic experience. I gained insight that the difference between a crazy person and a writer is that a crazy person talks to him/herself, but a writer also writes it down. I was no longer afraid to write, something I struggled with, especially during my years as a student. Words were not the enemy; they were my friends and my companions on this trip.

I wrote these words as I sat on my porch/office, my feet up on the table in front of me, late one night. I should have gone to bed, but the words continued to flow. They rolled into my notebook like the waves I could hear in the background. The constant drone of the crickets and frogs was punctuated every once in a while by the strange croak of what I guessed was a frog. It sounded like a deep male voice saying the word "crappy." I hoped that wasn't meant to be a reflection on my writing.

The flow of words finally stopped—like turning off a tap. I emerged from the torrent of words and finally noticed the halo of mosquitoes around me. A night of scratching—not words, but bites—would follow.

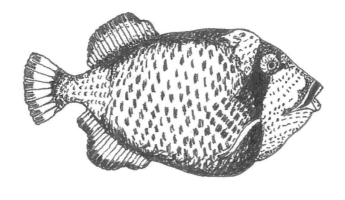

CHAPTER THIRTY-FIVE

Most days I was content to snorkel in the morning when the ocean was smoother and there was sporadic sunshine to illuminate the coral and fish. The snorkeling in front of the hotel was convenient although the coral was damaged by the fishing boats coming and going from their berths on the narrow beach. Also, sediment from a drainage canal coming down from the mountain had smothered some of the coral with a layer of brown sludge. By swimming over to an area in front of Wawa Wewe II, the visibility in the water improved. I could go when I wanted and stay as long as I wanted.

One morning, I sighted a fish whose coloring was a cross between a giraffe, leopard and zebra. Unlike other fish that darted and flashed about, this solitary fellow (he reminded me of Suki) stayed totally still on a piece of coral. I watched him for about ten minutes, and he didn't move. His bright yellow, ochre and black stripes and spots made him stand out on the smooth piece of grey coral like a floral umbrella in a sea of dark ones.

Moving on, I spotted a bigger fish that I named *elephant fish without a trunk*. He was chunky, almost as high as he was long and his yellow stubby tail was edged in black. He was slightly flat but not as flat as a flounder. He had startled me because of his size. He started poking at some branch coral. Perhaps this patch of coral was dead or damaged because he was able to excavate it easily. I watched in amazement as he broke off pieces with his snout and then used his mouth to pick them up and move them to one side. I could hear the crack of the coral as he broke off piece after piece. He worked methodically until he cleared an area about six inches square.

Many varieties of smaller fish swam nearby and made occasional darts to check elephant fish's progress. Having accomplished his task, he started feeding on whatever he had uncovered under the coral. Some of the braver small fish swarmed in to sample some of the delicacy. He snipped at the tails of a few that encroached too much on his excavated feast. I moved closer to see what the big attraction might be. Elephant fish held his ground, defiant that a larger rival was approaching his meal. He swung towards me to frighten me off as he had done with the small fish. He veered off before hitting me. Perhaps nearsighted, he didn't realize that I was bigger than him. He made the prudent choice of flight over fight. *My* nearsightedness prevented me from seeing what had caused this feeding frenzy. I backed off and he returned to his meal.

Gede, who worked on the reception desk, later helped identify my elephant fish as a Triggerfish. I consulted Wikipedia and it confirmed that the fish I'd seen was a Titan Triggerfish and that they were notoriously ill-tempered. An accompanying photograph showed a nasty bite received by a diver from a triggerfish's strong teeth.

I soon learned in my almost daily snorkeling forays that I should not always look down at the coral below me. By looking straight ahead and partially on a level with the water's surface, I was more likely to see larger fish and varieties that swam closer to the surface. I was spooked twice by ghostly needle fish, at least a foot long, which leisurely glided past me just under the surface. Another time, I was surprised by the fleeting glimpse of a large dull fish with a unicorn protuberance extending straight from its snout.

Each time I snorkeled, I saw different fish. There were black fish that looked like they had an orange ribbon tied around the spot where the body joined the tail. There was an aquamarine fish with an asymmetrical smudge of brilliant orange right behind its gills. There was a velvety black fish whose fins and tail were an iridescent turquoise on the reverse side.

I was trying to imprint into my memory the images of all the beautiful fish I saw. I tried sketching the shapes and colors when I went ashore, but my memory failed me each time. I tried finding photographs of tropical fish on the internet. Even then, I was useless at identifying the fish I'd seen underwater. Was that a long-nosed butterfly fish I'd sighted on a particular morning? I learned there were many varieties of butterfly fish with many different color combinations. One similar fish with a long tubular snout was a Moorish Idol. The name came from the Moors of Africa who purportedly believed the fish to be a bringer of happiness. Seeing them made *me* happy.

My attempts at videoing and photographing the fish failed. I'd fried one underwater camera on a previous vacation in Cozumel. I fried the second one on this trip to Bali the first time I used it underwater. Both times I forgot to check that the button holding the computer cable access hatch was in the locked position. My friends and family were forever spared the boredom of viewing murky, jerky underwater videos and photographs of tiny specks in the distance that might or might not be fish. I lost all the photos on the camera including ones I'd taken when I wasn't in the water.

I realized that there was no point in becoming a tropical fish expert, and I had no interest in competing with fellow snorkelers as to who had seen the most/best/rarest fish. Experiencing the visual beauty of the coral and fish was its own reward.

The coral in the bay in front of Pondok Vienna Beach was particularly stunning. The beach here was a combination of white and black sand and was very wide, unlike the narrow, rocky beach at Double One Villas. There, walking into the water involved the agony of stumbling over sharp, slippery rocks while large waves increased the risk of falling. The sheltered bay at Pondok Vienna Beach was a fifteen minute walk away with the added benefit of burning a few calories going up and down the steep hills on the way.

There were so many different varieties of magnificent coral. Flat areas of coral with a smooth surface looked like a painter's drop sheet after painting a rainbow-colored room. Pale pink finger coral jutted up against coral that looked like emerald green moss. Lacy, mauve fan coral swayed gently in the current. Overlapping toadstool coral was layered in shades of pink, orange and grey. Big round balls of coral had different textured surfaces. In some of the deep fissures of one type, prickly porcupine sea urchins were hiding. A grey coral looked like fingers with the nails painted with fluorescent blue nail polish.

There was pink cauliflower coral, mauve cauliflower coral, green broccoli coral, mottled brown and green coiled snake coral and Dijon mustard coral. There was grey coral that looked like suede from a distance, but up close the rippling surface was a living organism. I swam close to what appeared to be a piece of green fabric draped over the bumpy ocean floor. The fabric seemed to be edged by a light yellow border. That too was coral. This same type of coral, but grey, reminded me of the mold that sometimes grew on the surface of spoiled food in my refrigerator.

Although it was not colorful, there was a type of coral that was exquisite in form. It extended up from the sea bed like rosettes of fine porcelain cups. The edges were softly scalloped with some petals overlapping others. Some of them were like a single, open flower or chalice. Others formed multiple layers with the largest on the bottom, like a nest of slightly tipsy bowls. The surface of the petals looked smooth from a distance but up close was rough like an elephant's hide, with fine fissures and rivulets.

The smaller coral looked like rock gardens planted by a color-blind gardener. In one such garden, which extended for about fifteen feet in every direction, schools of orangey yellow fish shimmered like flakes of gold. In this cove, I discovered a long, needle fish, but unlike the ghostly grey ones I'd already seen, this one was sunshine yellow with a black ring near the end of his tail. I encountered a solitary, not very attractive, chunky fish with just a stub for a tail. I looked up once to discover schools of three-to-four-inch-long black fish companionably swimming along with me. One of them came to within a few inches of my outstretched hand. A light grey fish with catfish whiskers used them to rummage through a sandy spot looking for a meal. I was overwhelmed by the variety of fish and coral I was seeing just a few feet under the surface of the ocean. It was a miraculously beautiful underwater kingdom.

Even when the views were less than ideal, the sensation of floating, limbs relaxed, head down, sometimes being gently carried by the current, was a meditative experience. I felt one with nature and at peace with the world. I had overcome my childhood fear of underwater monsters.

Granted, there were times when I felt a rush of fear when the waves were high or the current unpredictable. It was the same feeling I experienced every time I stepped out on the ice to play hockey. I was a risk taker and I was brave.

"You really should play, you know."

My friend and fellow artist, Nancy, tried to convince me as we were working together in my basement studio. She had come to use my press to produce a series of woodcut prints.

"Now that Andrew can drive himself, how else are you going to spend all that extra time that you once spent on the road and in rinks? Besides, you've been watching him play for years so you know the game."

To me that was like saying, "So, you've watched Olympic diving for years — just get yourself up on that board and hurl yourself at the water." In hockey, though, the water was frozen and hard.

"I'm older than you and I love playing."

Indeed, Nancy was in her early fifties and was an inspiration as a mature hockey player. A bout with cancer a few years earlier had motivated her to start playing the game that she had always loved watching.

Nancy's quiet voice belied a strong will, and so I found myself, a few months later, asking her how to put on the assortment of hockey equipment that I'd lugged to the first game of the season. Most of the equipment were cast-offs from my son, but a large pair of shin pads were contributed by my boyfriend, who had the sense to stop playing in his twenties. The smell from the pile of equipment was a cross between that of a sweaty teenage boy and cat pee. Arthur, our cat, attracted by the musty male odor wafting from the open hockey bag in the basement, had added his own distinctive, pungent contribution. The gloves smelled particularly foul; that was probably why Andrew had discarded them. Until my parents bought me a new pair a few seasons later, my hands would stink after each game.

I nervously looked around the room at my fellow players, watching to see how they put on their equipment. Knowing nothing about appropriate equipment for female players, I'd brought one of Andrew's old jock straps and a molded plastic protection cup. I fumbled trying to put the two pieces together while the other women easily pulled on their "jills" that were built into a pair of shorts. The shorts also had Velcro strips that held up their hockey socks. I, meanwhile, was trying to find a dime in my purse to substitute for one of the missing rubber pieces in my son's tattered garter belt. How could men who played hockey ever consider garter belts as a sexy item of clothing after using them to hold up their smelly, holey hockey socks? Reluctant to invest much money in equipment, I was lucky that Andrew's old helmet and the skates he had worn when he was thirteen fit me perfectly.

The age range for this senior, recreational division of the Etobicoke Dolphins Girls Hockey League was eighteen and up. Most of the women looked to be in their twenties and thirties. Nancy and I seemed to be the only players in the up part of the age range.

"Whoa, whew, oops!"

I wasn't prepared for how different skating in boys' hockey skates would be from skating in women's figure skates. The curved end of the boys' skate blade required more skill to stay upright as opposed to the flat women's blade. I did discover that the hockey stick provided extra stability, not unlike a cane or crutch.

I made several interesting discoveries during that first game.

I needed a left-shooting stick, not a right-shooting stick.

A small pair of boys' shoulder and chest pads didn't provide adequate protection for slightly low-hanging breasts.

Playing as a forward (as Andrew did) required superior skating ability and physical stamina, neither of which I had.

An effective way to stop, in lieu of a figure skating pirouette, was simply to head either for the boards or another player.

Although women's recreational hockey could be fiercely competitive, it could also be extremely polite. "I really didn't mean to wipe you out," was usually accompanied by a helping hand.

Playing hockey is fun even when you don't actually touch the puck throughout the whole game.

I was either incredibly brave or massively foolhardy in starting to play hockey at the age of forty-five.

Chapter Thirty-Six

There were no spas in Amed dedicated solely to providing massages and beauty treatments. A few of the bigger hotels had names such as Puri Wirata Resort and Spa, but I didn't know if the spas were going concerns. Occasionally, a woman on the beach or one stopping at my porch asked if I wanted a massage.

After lunch at Wawa Wewe II one day, a woman sitting with a friend spoke to me.

"You like massage? Very special, Balinese style."

"Where would I have it?" I said.

She gestured to one of the two thatched-roof structures, slightly elevated by posts, which were located next to the beach. Until then, I'd assumed these huts were resting and meeting spots for the various young men who gathered there.

"How much?" I said.

"Very cheap. One hundred thousand rupiah."

It was worth spending twelve dollars to find out how this Balinese -style massage differed from the ones I'd already had.

"Okay, I'll be back soon," I told her.

When I returned, I saw that she'd taken a cushion from a lounge chair, covered it with a sarong and placed it on the wood floor of the platform. A boy of about fourteen, who was often on the beach selling toy replicas of the *jukung* to the rare visitor, wandered over near the hut. He obviously knew what was to come and didn't want to miss the show. The woman who had negotiated the massage deal deferred to her friend to do the massage. They seemed to be working in partnership. The one who could speak English made the sales pitch, and the quiet one was the masseuse. She indicated that I should remove my t-shirt. I wasn't wearing a bra, so I looked around for a towel or a length of fabric that could be used as a modesty shield. Then I looked over at the boy who had settled into a front row seat on the nearby stone wall. He had a big grin on his face. I turned my back on him, pulled my t-shirt over my head, and as quickly as I could manage lay face down on the cushion.

This Balinese style massage *was* a different experience from the ones I had in Ubud. Rather than the luxury of an elegant spa with scented oils and special juices, I lay on a lounge chair cushion in an open and simple bamboo structure beside a rocky beach, shooing houseflies away. And this time I had an audience.

The massage was a gentle one with no painful prodding of pressure points and knotted muscles. It was as thorough as the others, in that all of my body was worked on, but this was more relaxing. I was initially annoyed by the chatter between the two women, imagining they were arguing over the commission for the saleslady. Once they stopped, there was just the lapping of the waves and, of course, the crowing of roosters. Even knowing the boy was watching didn't bother me. The only thing that mattered was the pleasure generated by the rhythmic movement of the woman's hands.

I'd almost drifted off into oblivion when the woman indicated with her hands that I should turn over. I glanced to the right; my voyeur was still there. I gestured to the woman that I needed my t-shirt, which she had set aside out of my reach. Taking it, I clasped it to my breast, turned over onto my back and arranged the shirt to cover the floppy bits on my chest. The massage ended with the woman holding my head, gently kneading my cheeks, my temples and my skull. I now knew the meaning of "having someone in the palm of your hand." She could have asked me for anything, and I would have obliged. Perhaps it was a good thing she *couldn't* speak English.

Languorously, I turned my back on the boy and slipped on my t-shirt. I glided home by way of the beach accompanied by the scent of coconut oil. My body felt weightless, and not even the rocks on the beach seemed as hard and sharp on my tender feet as they once had.

CHAPTER THIRTY-SEVEN

Suki easily talked me into taking me to his friend/cousin/uncle's *warungs* for dinner. One such memorable evening, we were the only customers. About an hour later, another young Balinese man arrived with two Australian women who appeared to be sisters in their late thirties. They were in a celebratory mood because this was their last night in Bali. Suki enticed me there that particular evening with the promise of live music. A bongo drum and two guitars were sitting on a raised platform close to where Suki and I were sitting. First the bongo player arrived and started gently tapping out a rhythm. About ten minutes later, the two guitar players arrived and began to fuss with the strings and knobs. During this process, the three men chatted and joked. Tuning completed, they started to play soft, ballad music singing along in Balinese. Another man appeared carrying a tambourine and joined in. The tambourine looked like a toy—painted pink and shaped like a heart. A fourth man came and found a ribbed, glass soda bottle and a knife and added a percussive layer to the music. More men arrived, joining those already on the platform by sitting cross-legged on the floor. The guitars and bongo were passed to these new arrivals. Within an hour, there were twelve young men singing and sharing the instruments. Those without instruments lit cigarettes and smoked.

The owner of the *warung* brought large bottles of beer and glasses and placed them in the middle of the circle. The Australian women had by now joined the men on the platform. They also were sitting cross-legged on the floor, smoking cigarettes and drinking beer. Suki and I were invited to join the crowd on the platform, but we didn't move. I knew I couldn't sit like that for very long before my bum would hurt and my legs would go to sleep.

Plastic water bottles were added to the crowded circle accompanied by small shot glasses. The shot glasses were filled from the water bottles and passed around. It became obvious, as the songs got louder and the conversation more animated, that the water bottles didn't contain water. One of the Australian women was now leaning against the wall, and her friend/sister looked dangerously close to falling over. Suki and I were still seated at the table as onlookers rather than participants. As if in synch, we both knew it was time to leave, and the sound of music and laughter was soon drowned out by the roar of Suki's motorbike.

Two evenings later, we returned to another *warung* just two buildings over from the first. This one was owned by an uncle in the extended clan. Again, Suki had promised music. Halfway through the meal, the owner appeared and sat on the floor in front of a gamelan instrument. The pipes were of decreasing length and breadth and were made of hollow branches of bamboo, cut in half lengthwise. These were set in a bamboo frame. Across the front, facing us, a piece of curved wood was painted with a red and white flower pattern. The owner used two sticks with hammer heads to strike the bamboo reeds. This type of gamelan was similar to a marimba or a glockenspiel. Other gamelans are made of wood or metal and are more like drums.

Gamelan is an instrument played through improvisation rather than by following written music. Being the only customer and having shared a beer with Suki, I felt brave enough to ask the owner if I could try playing the instrument. What I thought was one long gamelan was really two shorter ones pushed together. The owner passed me a second set of striking sticks and our duet began. A sprightly little girl, the owner's daughter, joined our ensemble, improvising her own style of Balinese dancing. Since my musical talents are nonexistent, I left a generous tip to make up for subjecting the patient owner and his family to my performance.

A musical instrument in my past also represented pain rather than pleasure. The upright piano had been in John's family before being moved to our home. While he dithered and delayed making a decision about returning to the marriage or staying with his girlfriend, he didn't want to move the piano. For almost a year, its squat, solid presence in my living room fueled both my desperate hope that he might come back and my hatred of him for having left.

November 3, 1992

Finally confronted him at the hockey game and had my delusional dreams shattered. Again I thought the worst, said it and had it confirmed. Tracey moving in with him, Tracey not happy about having the kids, Tracey buying a car—everything going just fine for him. Exploded when I got home, called him asshole and tried to scratch it in piano. The symbol of hope (and despair) is finally going but not without its graffiti.

December 21, 1992

Lots of anger this morning when piano was moved. As usual, logistics were not for my convenience, and I was shaking with rage.

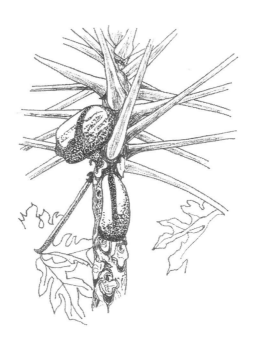

CHAPTER THIRTY-EIGHT

By the third week of my stay in Bali, it was obvious by the fit of my clothes that my activity level had not kept pace with my caloric intake. I needed to get more exercise than just floating along in the water while snorkeling or walking up and down flights of steps. My Frommer's guide sang the praises of trekking. In particular, it praised the merits of trekking up several of Bali's mountains to view the sunrise. Some of these treks involved at least four hours of walking up a steep trail in the dark to reach the top of the mountain at daybreak. Never an early riser, I decided to pass on one of those treks.

Double One Villas was located near the bottom of a mountain covered by bushes and trees. According to a healthy and energetic older German couple I'd met at a *warung*, there was a path up the mountain to a spot near the top where the view of the fishing village and ocean below was spectacular. They had given me rudimentary instructions on accessing the path.

I started out at ten o'clock in the morning wearing my running shoes, shorts, t-shirt and Panama hat. I'd even unearthed my glasses so I could see where I was going and admire the view from the top of the mountain. I carried an umbrella, for the inevitable daily deluge, and a blue nylon bag containing my camera, sunscreen, a granola bar, a bottle of water, mosquito repellant and toilet paper. I was ready for anything: rain, sun, hunger, thirst, mosquitoes and the call of nature.

I informed Eko at the reception desk that I was going trekking— in case anyone missed me.

"Where?" he asked.

"Up there." I pointed up at the mountain.

He shook his head. By now he was aware of the antics of this crazy, older woman from Canada.

"Very hard," he said. "Need guide."

"Not necessary. I won't get lost. I'll be able to see the water, and I'll just head for it if I'm not sure where I am." I said this with more confidence than was warranted, considering my lack of navigational skills.

Within five minutes of walking along the road, two different men on motorbikes asked if I needed a driver.

"No," I said with conviction, "I'm going trekking."

One of the men confirmed the existence of a small road, off the bigger road, that would lead to a concrete path ending at a trail that would take me up the mountain. I thanked him and walked on.

He had said to take the first left turn onto the smaller road. This road looked more like a steep driveway leading to someone's home rather than a real road. But it was the first left turn and up I went. I passed three men building a house on a steep incline.

They were close enough to hear them yell, "Cigarette, cigarette."

I yelled back, "No, I don't smoke," knowing they would understand the first word if not the rest.

Around the bend, the road appeared to end at some cell phone towers. It must just be a service road for these towers, I thought, and retraced my steps down the steep driveway and past the builders. I walked along the main road looking for the proper turnoff.

A man coming towards me on a motorbike stopped to ask the inevitable question, "Need driver?"

We recognized each other about the same time. He was one of the young men who hung out at the beach trying to sell the toy *jukung*. I was relieved it wasn't the boy who had enjoyed witnessing my massage.

"No thanks, I don't need a driver. I'm walking up the mountain." I didn't sound as confident about my trek as I had earlier.

"Path hard to find. You need guide. I take you."

"How much?" I asked. By now I was losing my resolve to find my own way.

"What you want to give," he replied.

He, like Suki, had learned that sometimes it is more lucrative to leave the price to the buyer's discretion. He was a personable young man, tall and skinny, and his English was passable. He became my trekking guide. He also became my Sherpa in the ascent of this miniature Everest because he insisted on carrying my blue bag and red umbrella.

We headed back along the main road in the direction that I'd just come. We turned up the steep driveway I'd recently gone up and then came down. I thought I might have heard some laughter from the three builders who I was now passing for the third time. The driveway did end at the cell phone towers as I'd guessed earlier. Hidden around behind a small utility building was a narrow concrete path heading up the hill.

My guide's name was Jana, he was twenty years old, and he was Suki's cousin. The concrete path got steeper and steeper.

"Jana, please slow down," I said.

Unlike his cousin, he did slow his pace, and he waited for me to catch up so we could walk together. After climbing for about fifteen minutes, he indicated that a dirt path branching off the concrete path was the route to his home on the neighboring mountain.

"That looks like a long way. Can you ride your motorbike along the path?" I asked.

"Rain make path dangerous for bike. Leave bike here and walk."

About two-thirds of the way up the mountain, I was breathing heavily and the back of my t-shirt was wet with sweat.

"Jana, I need to stop for a minute. I'm not used to trekking when it's so hot," I said.

"Soon place for rest. Not far." He pointed up the path and kept walking.

This *must* be Suki's cousin because they shared the same sadistic tendencies. He was right. Over the next rise and at the end of the paved path was a resting pavilion. It was similar in style to the massage hut on the beach, was much bigger and had a raised tiled floor. It was the equivalent of a rest stop on a super highway. It even had a small concrete outhouse, but unlike highway rest stops, a sturdy padlock signaled that it wasn't for public use.

"Who owns all this?" I asked gesturing to the structures and the land surrounding them.

"Farmer own but sell to rich man from Java. Rich man own big villa. Down there." He pointed to the small fishing village at the base of the mountain.

"This place, *bale bengong*, and path made by man from Java. He comes to see ocean. Find cool air. He plant this," he said, pointing to a simple garden on one side of the resting platform. "That papaya, kiwi, lime."

"I wondered what they were. I make pictures of flowers and trees; I draw them," I said.

Finding out that I was interested in plants, he showed me little plots on the mountain where pumpkin, soybeans and chili peppers were growing. These tiny gardens, tucked in among the wild bushes and vegetation, could have been easily overlooked.

"What about the farmer who sold this land to the rich man from Java?" I asked.

Jana replied sadly, "He waste money on *arak* and rooster fight."

Those damn noisy roosters were partly to blame for the farmer's downfall. Like some people who strike it rich by winning a big lottery prize, the farmer had spent it all on transitory pleasures.

News traveled fast in Amed. Suki found out that I'd hired his cousin as a trekking guide. I justified it by explaining that I'd told Jana that Suki was my official driver and that giving my trekking business to his cousin wasn't a bad thing.

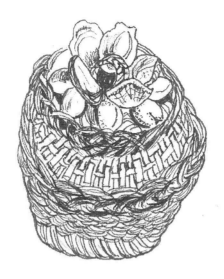

Chapter Thirty-Nine

I was down to my last four days in Amed. I'd finally decided to move on when Eko told me that the circulating pump on the pool was broken. I found four of the staff sitting on the steps to the reception area discussing the broken part that one of them held. I took that as a bad omen and informed Eko that I would be leaving on Saturday, four days hence. To my surprise, when I was passing the pool on my way to breakfast the next morning, I saw that the motor had been either fixed or replaced, reinstalled, and the water jets were gurgling again.

Suki knew he had only three days left to extract as much money from me as he could before he had to find another customer. I was, again, the only customer at Double One Villas. Business was bad at all the hotels and *warungs*. Low-season vacancy rates were high and the lack of opportunity to earn income was hard on everyone. Running out of snorkeling destinations and knowing that I enjoyed trekking and nature, Suki suggested a ride to one of the nearby mountains to see the rice fields followed by a trek to a spring where the water was considered holy by people in the surrounding villages. It wasn't a tour that would be of interest to many tourists. It was off the beaten path, way off, and there was no mention of it in my guide book. It seemed to be a special place only for the local people.

The name of the natural spring, *yeh masem*, translated into sour water. It was purported to have special refreshing properties if splashed on the face in the morning. Some of the older local people even drank it for its restorative powers. Not wanting to miss out on an opportunity to visit this possible fountain of youth (I could use its rejuvenating powers), I agreed to let Suki take me there.

Leaving the coastal road, we rode through an incredibly beautiful, fertile valley, the road following what might be considered either a small river or a large stream. We were going up gradually, the ascent not half as precipitous as most of the other rides we had taken. Changes in the river level were marked by a series of gentle waterfalls. The rushing water was bordered on both sides by rice fields dotted with bamboo huts and strings of fluttering fabric.

We passed people carrying huge bundles of fallen branches on their heads, and also women balancing sacks of rice. We approached an old wizened man and woman bent over by the weight of large bundles of green plants. They carried curved, cutting scythes in their hands.

"What are those plants?" I asked Suki.

"Food for cows," he replied.

There were few other motorbikes and no cars. The scene looked like a picture from a history book depicting rural life from a time long gone.

A roughly lettered sign on a scrap of wood shaped like an arrow was inscribed "5 HOLY SPRINGS." I hoped the five didn't refer to the number of miles we had to walk in order to reach the spring. The arrow pointed down a path that ran beside the wall of a family compound. There were no parking lots, no hawkers and no official or ad hoc guides. This was Bali at its best—unhurried, peaceful, picturesque and free of hassles.

The motorcycle excursion had covered relatively flat territory. The trek part didn't. There was no stone or cement path, just a well-traveled dirt path that became steep and challenging. I'd worn my leather walking sandals. They had finally dried after being used as wading shoes on the trek to the large waterfall. They had not fallen apart, but the leather was slightly stretched and wrinkly. Unwilling to get them wet again, I'd stuck my flip-flops in the blue bag I carried on my back. Suki, as usual, forged ahead at his own athletic and nimble pace. Finally, glancing back to see if I'd kept up with him, he noticed the bag on my back and offered to carry it. He probably hoped that by lessening my load, I would be able to keep up with him better.

Soon we needed to cross a stream. He told me to put on my flip-flops. The path resumed across the stream and became steep again. Rocks served as stepping stones, the earth between them wet and slippery. Flip-flops make adequate wading shoes, but they are *not* rock-climbing shoes.

I clutched at roots and bushes on either side of the path to steady myself. We approached a section where the earth and water had combined to form a mud bog. Suki pointed out the red color of the mud, which reminded me of the color of the soil in Prince Edward Island. The tops of a few rocks stuck up above the surface of the mud, but the tops were pointed, not flat and were positioned too far apart. I aimed one flip-flopped foot at a rock, slipped off the edge and landed ankle deep in the goopy mess. I lost my balance, and the second foot followed the first. I tried lifting a foot. The flip-flop was sucked deeper into the mud, and my foot came up bare. I rummaged in the muck to rescue my sandal, and I was careful to grip the other one with my toes to extract it from the mud.

"Suki, come back. I need help," I shouted to the rapidly disappearing figure on the path ahead.

Suki turned but made no move to come to my assistance.

"I need water to wash the slimy mud off my feet and flip-flops."

"Water ahead," he yelled back at me.

I stumbled forward on the uneven path. Now my footing was even more tenuous because of the mud-slicked surface of the flip-flops, the mud acting like a lubricant that made my feet slide out. I worried that the twisting motion of my feet would cause the toe piece to come apart from the sole. I was relieved when we reached the stream again where I could wash my feet and the flip-flops. Preparing for bed that evening, I looked at my toenails and noticed that they were still stained from the mud. A long swim in the pool and a shower hadn't removed the persistent orange tint. That burnt sienna tone, which made my toenails look like ancient artifacts, would prove to be one of the more lasting souvenirs of my trip to Bali.

We followed the stream and eventually came to a clearing containing a resting platform, a small stone temple and a pipe, water running from it, sticking out of a stone wall. We had arrived at the holy spring. Suki knelt and splashed water from the pipe over his head and face. I took my turn.

"Drink," he said.

I hesitated, wondering if I was at risk of contracting some horrendous disease from untreated water. A few drops couldn't hurt. The water was sour in a tangy way. It tasted not unpleasant, rather like weak lemonade. Suki filled a large water bottle that he had brought with him. I made a small contribution to a donation box fixed to a post of the resting platform. The box was directly below an offering shelf painted with a colorful flower pattern. The locals had left their miniature, woven baskets filled with rice, slices of fruit and flower petals. The tourists were expected to leave an offering of the monetary variety.

On the return journey, we detoured through the rice fields and stopped at some banana trees, where I posed for a photograph. This route took us past a tiny farm where a father and son appeared to be leveling some soil.

"Are they preparing the land for a garden plot?" I asked.

"No," Suki replied, "He makes ground flat to build house. Today ceremony for blessing house."

When I was taking a photograph of Suki at the holy water spring, he asked if we could have a print made of it.

"Sure," I said. "Is there a printer at Double One Villas that we can use?"

"No," he said, "Internet café."

Suki was somewhat vain. He selected three photographs of himself from among the hundreds of digital photographs on my camera. Two were shots of him wearing his sunglasses, which he had purposely donned during the photo shoot, and one was of him on his motorcycle. He grudgingly accepted my choice of one to print. I'd taken it soon after we met when I'd discovered him sitting on a lounge chair near the beach whittling the hull of a toy *jukung*. He'd chosen only photographs of himself (none included me), and he wanted them all printed on the largest paper size. Did he have four girlfriends who would all receive one of his photographs or would they be used to market his services? I hesitated about authorizing the printing until I learned that they would cost only one dollar each. We agreed they would be part of the payment for that morning's trek guiding services.

While the photographs were being printed, I wandered outside to look at the open-air shop across the street. It was mostly for the local people. There were two birds in bamboo cages suspended from tree branches in a shady bower, their song contributing musical notes to the pleasant scene.

Almost immediately, a girl of about four trotted up, hands extended. Each tiny hand held an exquisite little basket. In her right hand was a simple one woven from palm leaves like the offering baskets I'd seen everywhere. The lid was decorated with seed beads. The second one was more intricate, woven from very fine bamboo reeds. The top of this box was embellished with sea shells glued to resemble the petals of a flower. I was charmed, both by the little boxes and by the little girl who had remained silent during my inspection of the boxes. I removed the lid on the more intricate one and discovered a white granular substance wrapped in a piece of clear plastic.

That was the cue for the mother, who was hovering nearby, to approach and announce in English, "Salt."

I'd read in my guide book that sea salt was one of the local products.

"How much?" I asked the mother.

"Twenty thousand rupiah," she replied.

I found the money in the pouch at my waist. The mother now sported a big smile, not having expected an instant sale without bargaining. I was in a good mood—perhaps the holy water from the spring had a bewitching effect—and I considered the price, equivalent to about two dollars, to be more than fair. I had a souvenir small enough to squeeze into my suitcase. It contained a local product, the salt, and was decorated with shells that would remind me of my magical snorkeling experiences. It was also a pretty example of a handmade lidded box, and even better, it was offered to me by a lovely child with a shy smile.

I had a collection of other miniature boxes at home, including two made from birch bark and porcupine quills by First Nation Canadians, an octagonal one made from a dark tropical wood and a lidded basket from South Africa ingeniously woven from colored telephone wire.

News traveled fast about the customer that bought without bargaining. From out of nowhere, three women appeared, thrusting towards me woven trays displaying many baskets and also larger plastic bags of the local salt.

One woman was particularly aggressive saying, "You promise, you promise, you buy, you buy!" in a way that guaranteed I wouldn't make a purchase from her. Sending a child is perhaps a classic and questionable sales technique, but it was not done in a threatening or aggressive way so I felt good about my purchase.

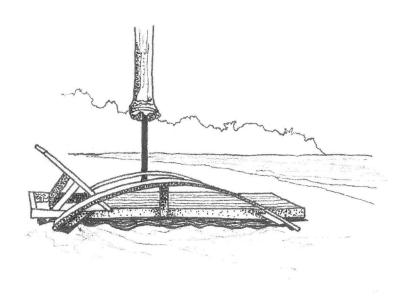

CHAPTER FORTY

On my last full day in Amed, I walked to Pondok Vienna Beach where the snorkeling had revealed large coral, a marvelous variety of fish and where the beach was broad and sandy. I was met by the man, similar in looks to Graham Greene (the First Nations actor), who'd rented me a lounge and umbrella for twenty thousand rupiah on a previous visit. He looked at me blankly when I tried to hand him the same amount.

"Fifty thousand," he said.

"The last time I paid you twenty thousand. Besides, I only need one lounge chair, not two, and I'm staying for only two hours at the most."

I was finally getting good at this bargaining game. I held my ground with the money in my outstretched hand. He looked at the money, looked me in the eye, realized I was more stubborn than he, smiled, touched my arm in a gesture of concession and took the money.

As he opened the tattered and sun-bleached beach umbrella, I casually said, "I might have forgotten my snorkeling t-shirt here the last time. Did you see it?"

He shook his head.

"Perhaps I'm mistaken. I do have a terrible memory." I smiled at him. "No great loss."

When I came out of the water later, the t-shirt was draped on the lounge chair next to mine.

As I was snorkeling, I raised my head and was startled by a large moving shape just below the surface nearby. I squinted to try to see if this was a large enough fish to consider me as his lunch. My distance vision is dicey at the best of times, but I realized the long black tail of the sea monster were snorkeling fins. By now, I was used to snorkeling alone, but when I saw the man begin to tread water to adjust his mask, I also removed my snorkel and mask so I could talk. I wanted to share my enthusiasm for the dazzling scene below the surface.

I blurted out, "Isn't this snorkeling amazing?"

"Right you are." I recognized his Australian accent.

We began a fifteen minute conversation while treading water. He was checking the water for his wife who was seven months pregnant.

"Have you noticed a strong current here?" he asked.

"Today, there is little or no current," I said. "But one day I snorkeled here, there was a moderate current. Maybe it depends on the tide direction and how strong the wind is."

"What direction was it flowing?" he asked.

I pointed.

Acknowledging my gesture, he said, "Then it's best for my wife to get into the water at the other end of the beach. She can be carried along by the current, get out at the far end and walk back."

I was impressed by his concern for his wife and his ingenuity in deciding on a plan that would allow them to snorkel together despite her advanced pregnancy. I was enjoying my conversation with the Aussie and he didn't seem in a hurry to resume his snorkeling.

"When my daughter was seven months pregnant, she loved being in the water. The buoyancy made her feel light and comfortable," I said.

The effort of treading water to stay afloat was tiring, and I asked what I really wanted to know. "Where's the best place you've ever snorkeled?"

"My job has taken me all over the Indo-Pacific Ocean. There's good snorkeling off many of the islands there," he replied.

When pressed, he narrowed his choices down to Tonga, Fiji and Western Samoa. The last destination had the added attraction of beautiful landscape, friendly people and cheap accommodation, just like Bali.

"Don't go to American Samoa," he advised. "Too much development and too expensive."

I had what I wanted from him—my next snorkeling destination. I released him from the job of socializing and treading water at the same time. His wife, watching from the beach, must have wondered if her husband was being lured away by a beautiful mermaid, although one with a yellow snorkel protruding from her head. In reality, he'd just been detained by an old sea hag.

Chapter Forty-One

It was my final breakfast at Double One Villas. As I came down the steep stone stairs to the dining area, I looked straight ahead at the view of the glistening ocean rather than looking down at my feet like I usually did. I was cautious after another guest had taken a tumble one rainy evening on the slippery stone surface. Fishermen were bringing in their boats. The colorful *jukung*, made entirely of wood and bamboo, were heavy, and it took five men to hoist them onto the beach, one on the bow and four with the curved part of the outriggers on their shoulders. It would have been a good day for snorkeling—a clear sky and a flat ocean. It hadn't rained for the last four days, a mixed blessing, since the previous day I'd received my first sunburn.

My compulsion to write had eased because rather than writing, I was reading. I'd made a conscious decision before leaving home not to bring a novel to read. I knew that would distract me from making art and writing. I was helped in my resolve when the only book written in English in the ad hoc lending library located on a single shelf in the dining area was a tattered and stained copy of Charles Dickens' "Nicholas Nickelby," the pages brown and brittle with age. I made the mistake of checking the shelf again just before I left Amed. There was a new donation. It was a book I'd always wanted to read, a 1994 Giller prize winner by Canadian author M.G. Vassanji, "The Book of Secrets." Picking it up, I discovered that some of the pages were loose. Further inspection revealed no missing pages. If there had been pages missing, I would have interpreted that as a sign to put the tempting book back on the shelf.

Sitting by the pool, I opened the cover, the paper flaccid in the humid air and fell into the world of Alfred Corbin as he wrote a diary of his experiences of traveling to and living in Kenya in the early twentieth century. Although it was a novel with fictional characters, I felt an immediate resonance with this book about an exotic and strange culture.

Write or read? Making the decision wasn't easy. Once made, the choice to read erased my desire to write. How could I possibly come close to emulating the tumble of words that were so descriptive of that time and place? Should I leave the book behind in Amed or bring it with me? In the end, I brought it with me and put it away like a forbidden treat to enjoy its promise of escape when I returned to Canada. Knowing my lack of resolve in regards to dark chocolate and good books—only one more square, only one more page—I hid the book away in my suitcase.

At my final dinner with Suki, he was less his taciturn self.

"Need new motorbike," he said. "Not strong enough." He gestured to his vehicle parked beside the stairs to the *warung* where we were eating.

"Yes, we did slow down on some of those big hills," I acknowledged.

"New have automatic shift," he continued.

"Why would you need that?" I asked.

"I rent motorbike to tourists. They not rent with old gears."

He was branching out in his entrepreneurial endeavors—motorcycle rental in addition to motorcycle driver. He'd not had much luck with me in the other type of service he offered.

"I sell old one. Get money. Need more money for new. Less to pay each month."

Who knew Suki had such a practical grasp of the economics of buying and selling motorcycles? It sounded as if he was asking his Canadian mother to help with the purchase. I listened but—as in some similar situations with Andrew—made no commitments.

The sky was clear, the moon spotlight-bright during the motorcycle ride back to Double One Villas. The next night there was to be a full moon. My astrological sign is Cancer, the moon child. My nickname when I was younger was Luna, not without just cause. I'd started to enjoy the motorcycle drives, particularly that idyllic evening. The scent of lightly fragranced oil wafted from Suki's hair. My hands held him just below his hips, resting on the curve of his firm young butt. My legs were spread, straddling the black leather seat, feet supported by the collapsible footrests. As we climbed one of the steeper hills, I looked back to the fishing village nestled softly in the cove.

Since it was my last night there, I suggested to Suki that he should try opening the email account I'd helped him to create on my netbook.

"See if Gede will let you use the hotel's computer."

Gede, the last staff member on duty other than the night watchman, Suki and I crowded into the office that was about the size of a telephone booth. I sat in the only chair to start the computer training session. I showed both of them how to access Suki's account then I had Suki try on his own. With Gede's help, he was successful and had a big, uncharacteristic smile on his face.

"I'll send you an email from my netbook and you try to open it," I said.

Not only did he manage to open and read my email, but to my surprise, I received a reply in return. There were only a few words in the message, but it meant that Suki, with Gede's help, had mastered email.

By now it was ten o'clock, time for Gede to turn off the lights in the reception area and lock the office. Suki followed me down the hill.

Date: Saturday, October 28, 2006
"Susan and Marcio invite you to their annual Halloween Party"

Should I go, who'll be there, what should I wear? The e-invite trig-gered these questions. Susan was an artist friend and her husband was from South America, so the party promised to be lively. The list of invi-tees included mutual friends and also Susan and Marcio's South Ameri-can friends.

With the first two questions answered, the third proved to be the most difficult. The attraction of Halloween parties was that they allowed you to dress-up and be a different person. For women, that might be a sexy nurse or rock star and for men, an equally sexy pirate or superhero. It offered an opportunity for me to play a role other than that of daughter or mother. I phoned my daughter for ideas because she'd always come up with original and creative ideas for her own Halloween costumes, even when she was a young girl.

"What did you wear last year? All I remember is that it was some-thing really clever."

"All my costumes were clever," she said. "Last year I was a Freudian Slip."

I dug to the bottom of my underwear drawer, searching through the mass of cotton panties, camisoles and pantyhose that were intertwined like tree roots. Finally, I found what I was looking for—a black, knee-length slip. It was from a deceased aunt and looked to be from the fifties. Both the bodice and the hem were edged with a pleated frill of lace and it had skinny satin straps.

I tried it on. The close-fitting, slinky nylon fabric was flattering, but the transparency of the fabric was more provocative than I dared to wear, even on Halloween. I plunged back into the drawer finally pulling out a black satin padded bra. This helped make my costume less revealing and at the same time, enhanced it. My nipples were now camouflaged by the padding and the bra's under-wire construction created a subtle cleavage in the v-neckline of the slip's bodice. Surviving the night in the tight cinch of the bra would be a challenge.

I untangled the pantyhose from the rest of the underwear but couldn't find either black ones or tights. I knew I had to find something to wear on the lower half of my body underneath the translucent slip. An avalanche of leggings and pants tumbled down from the top shelf of my closet as I pulled out the black cotton leggings that were on the bottom of the pile. They were a hold-over from the 1980s and had gone in and out of fashion several times since then. I pulled them on and stood back to assess my costume in the mirror. The addition of the leggings made my costume somewhat more modest but slightly wonky. I looked even more eccentric when I put on high-heeled black sandals.

The top drawer of my dresser contained an assortment of jewelry and odds and ends of things that were probably useless but that I didn't want to throw away. Artists tend to be pack rats. The plastic nametag that I was rummaging for was still there. I slipped out the name card, wrote FREUD in large block letters on the back and slipped it back in the holder with my new identity visible.

To add a glamorous note to my naughty/nice/weird outfit, I donned a rhinestone necklace and matching dangly earrings and applied a surplus of make-up. Finally, I topped my ensemble with a black, rabbit fur coat that had been an inheritance from a different aunt. The coat was also fifties style with oversized, cuffed sleeves and a shawl collar that I turned up to touch the edges of my blonde hair. I hoped the few small holes in the dried skin of the fur were not too obvious.

Arriving at the party, I was tempted to leave the coat on, having lost my courage about revealing my provocative costume. I reluctantly gave up custody of the protective coat and soon discovered that my clever outfit served as an icebreaker with the other guests.

"What are you supposed to be?" was repeated constantly by both

friends and strangers.

I pointed to my nametag, FREUD, and then to my slip, hoping that most people would make the connection between the two. Some of them did just not "get" it. With each glass of white wine I drank, I felt less conspicuous. The music became louder and the enticing rhythm soon had the living room full of dancing couples.

"Do you salsa?"

The soft voice was almost inaudible above the intense beat of the music. I turned to see a young Arabian sheikh outfitted in a dressing gown with a head covering made with a pillow case held on by a length of cord.

"No thanks," I said, "I'll have some food later."

Without acknowledging my mistake, he took my hand and led me to a spot in the hallway next to the living room that by this time was packed with couples caught up in the seductive moves of the salsa. Holding one of my hands, he skillfully circled my waist with his other arm and drew me firmly to him. His grip was close and strong. Even in my inebriated state, I was able to match the movements of his body in the increasingly more sensual moves of the dance. He turned me so my back was against his front and his hands dropped to my thighs and our hips moved together.

My face felt hot and red from the heat of the dance, the heat of the room and the effects of white wine on an empty stomach. Seeing my flushed face and feeling the sweat-moistened fabric of my slip, he wordlessly opened the front door and led me out into the chilly autumn air. He drew me against him and put his arms around my shoulders so that the voluminous sleeves of the bathrobe provided some warmth for my bare skin. As his face came towards mine, I had just a glimpse of the moon over his shoulder before our lips connected.

My body responded to the kiss, but my befuddled brain managed to formulate a warning, "Be careful, it's almost a full moon. No Freudian Slips tonight!"

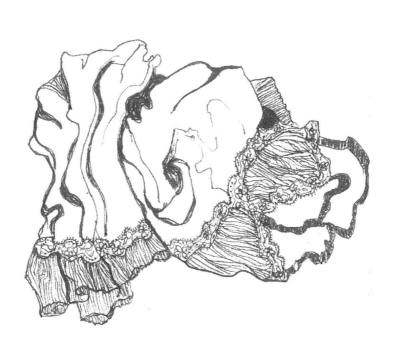

Chapter Forty-Two

Most of my breakfasts at Double One Villas were served by Wanda, a sweet, moon-faced woman. There was the choice of two standard breakfasts included with the lodging price. I'd settled into the habit of having the same food every morning. At home, it was coffee, orange juice and oatmeal topped with a sliced banana and yogurt. In Amed, my breakfast started with strong Balinese coffee, without milk, accompanied by a plate containing three varieties of sliced, fresh fruit. The fruit selection varied, based on what was available that particular day: pineapple, banana, watermelon or papaya. This was followed by a banana or pineapple crepe made with rice flour. Wedges of lime garnished both the fruit plate and the crepe. I squeezed the juice on my crepe and drizzled it with the slightly runny honey that Wanda served in a small bowl. I'd learned to place the empty sugar packages and the empty honey bowl on the other side of the table so that the tiny ants that were always present would have their breakfast on the other side of the table and not share the food on my plate.

I am not a gourmand. I do appreciate a variety of fresh food, and I am willing to try new food. Whenever possible, especially in Amed since it was a fishing village, I ordered fish for dinner. I ate a lot of rice—hence my concern with weight gain—either plain or as part of a mixture. One rice dish was *mi goreng*, a fried rice dish containing vegetables, chicken and the occasional shrimp, all topped by a fried egg. *Gado gado*, a similar dish, was topped by a hardboiled egg, and instead of meat, it was made of fried tofu and tempeh. Tempeh was a soybean cake that reminded me of Rice Crispy squares without the marshmallows. *Gado gado* contained vegetables and bean sprouts and was topped with peanut sauce before the egg was added.

Because there were so few customers at Double One Villas, the kitchen wasn't well stocked. I often had to make alternative menu choices. Finally, I stopped asking for particular dishes and instead asked what they *did* have.

One food that I often had for lunch was tomato soup. I commented to Made how tasty it was. He revealed his recipe to me. He sautéed tomatoes, onion, garlic and some spices and then pureed them in a blender. The blender appeared to be the most utilized appliance in Bali. All the fruit drinks were made by plopping fruit in a blender with some water. Made was also an entrepreneur as well as a waiter/cook. He presented me with his card. His business appeared to be a pyramid selling scheme.

At Taksu Spa and Restaurant in Ubud, as well as enjoying the "Raw Cuisine," I sampled a tasty pudding made of pureed (there's that blender again) avocado and chocolate.

At Pondok Vienna Beach where I snorkeled, the guacamole was served with shrimp chips. They were served hot from the deep fat fryer and were substantial and tasty.

At Wawa Wewe II, I discovered that the salad called "The Works" (an appropriate name) made for a substantial and economical lunch. Also on the menu there was a jaffle. It consisted of two pieces of white bread filled with any combination of meat, cheese, bacon or tomato, which was then toasted in a sandwich press that sealed the edges.

On the "Non Alkohic" section of the menu at Wa La Wa Café in Amed was a "Shaolin Teample." On the same menu in the "Western Food" section was a "Frencsisdle." The waiter said it was a sausage rolled in noodles and fried. I decided to pass.

CHAPTER FORTY-THREE

I said my goodbyes to the staff at Double One Villas without the hugs that might have been appropriate in a different culture. In public, I'd never seen people kissing or hugging one another or even holding hands. The only body contact I noticed, other than sharing a motorcycle seat, was that of mothers or grandmothers carrying babies. Even that contact appeared to be for religious reasons. Before a special ceremony when they were one hundred and five days old, babies were always carried so they didn't come in contact with the evil spirits associated with the ground.

As we set out from Amed in the rented car, Nyoman, Suki and I saw many people wearing ceremonial clothing. I'd now learned about the distinctive headwear worn by the men. There were, as I understood it, three styles of what the Balinese called an *udeng*. There were small ones that wrapped around the head leaving the crown of the head uncovered. Sometimes one end of the fabric was flipped up into a triangle. This was the type of *udeng* I noticed most often. Then there was one that covered the full head, the *pemangku*, and there was a big one, the *pedanda*, which was worn for the bell ceremony. It was similar in style but smaller than the turbans worn by men of the Sikh religion. There were different colors for different ceremonies. White was worn in temple ceremonies, black for cremations, and the most colorful ones, or as Made described them, the "prettiest" *udeng*, were worn for weddings.

The day of our transit was a school holiday for the children and a day of ceremonies, a celebration of the full moon that night. Nyoman asked if we could pick up his wife from his village, Culik, where I'd witnessed the *ogoh-ogoh* festivities. We were to drop her in Amlapura, the destination of my rain-soaked drive with Suki, where she would visit her mother on this special holiday.

"Of course," I said.

We stopped in front of a shop. Nyoman tooted the horn several times and out scurried two small girls and a woman with a baby boy in her arms. Nyoman opened the car door, and his family piled into the back seat forcing Suki to share his exclusive territory.

"I'm Lorna," I said, turning to greet these new arrivals.

Nyoman stared straight ahead and started the car without introducing his wife and children. The wife smiled broadly at me, the little girls giggled shyly and the round-faced baby boy glared at me. The oldest girl, maybe six years old, was festively dressed in a cherry red dress patterned with tiny colored flowers.

Not a sound was heard on the thirty minute trip to Amlapura. I was enjoying the beautiful mountain landscape that I'd missed on my first wet trip by motorcycle. The children were so quiet that I turned to check to see if everyone was okay. The baby was sleeping peacefully against his mother's breast, and the girls were looking out the windows. For them, this drive in a car might have been a rare luxury. I'd seen many families with multiple members jammed on a single motorcycle.

School children who were not lucky enough to have either parents or siblings pick them up by motorcycle were transported home to their villages in the Balinese equivalent of a yellow school bus. These were basically large pick-up trucks with the cargo space enclosed by high railings. The children stood, wedged in tightly so more of them could be packed in and they wouldn't fall down. There was no roof to provide protection from either the blazing sun or the sometimes torrential downpours. As these "school buses" passed me on my walks to the snorkeling at Pondok Vienna Beach, the sound of chattering young voices both proceeded and followed the vehicle.

Near Amlapura, we pulled into the parking lot of the tourist attraction that I'd asked Nyoman to stop at on our way to Sanur. Suki and I got out and Nyoman said he would return for us after he had dropped off his wife and children.

The place was called *Tirta Gangga*, which, when prompted, Suki said meant *large pool of clean water*. Subsequent research on the internet translated it as *blessed water of the Ganges*. As a tour guide, he left much to be desired. It was also known as the *Royal Water Palace*. After I bought our entrance tickets, we walked through the opening in the stone wall that was typical of most entrances to compounds. The doorway looked like a pyramid temple that had been chopped in two, the pieces pushed to the side to create an entryway. This type of gate was called a *candi bentar* and symbolized the mountain where the gods lived.

The scene that greeted us was like a formal English garden, but one that had been transported to a level plateau on the side of a lush, rainforest mountain. We walked between two pools that were approximately thirty feet wide by one hundred and fifty feet long. They were about five feet deep. The one on our left was filled with solid orange carp and others mottled in myriad combinations of orange, white and grey. The other pond was dotted with ornate sculptures of beasts and water creatures. There was an eleven-tier water fountain and on the far side of the ponds a temple gaily adorned in banners and flowers to mark the auspicious holiday of the full moon.

I glanced apprehensively at Suki because he had told me to bring a bathing suit to swim in one of the pools. I didn't fancy swimming with the carp, and it didn't seem appropriate to cavort among the sculpture in the other pool. Suki marched forward, not checking to see if I was still following him. He approached another stone wall with the *candi bentar* entry portal, shook his head from side to side to the ticket taker there and proceeded in. I surrendered my ticket to the outstretched hand and walked through the gate. Relieved, I saw that there was a bathing pool. A squat building with changing rooms was located at one end of the pool. When I came out, Suki had already settled into his customary cross-legged position on the grass in the shade of a bush, smoking and text messaging.

I was the only occupant of this huge pool. There were no steps to access the water, just a shallow ledge. I stepped in and the water was refreshingly cool. The bottom and sides of the pool were constructed of blocks of dark grey volcanic rock. Possibly through lack of use, the bottom of the pool was kind of yucky and slippery with a layer of algae. It reminded me of the bottom of the untended aquarium tank that had languished in Andrew's boyhood bedroom. Spring water was spouting from two sources, a metal pipe and the mouth of a carved stone dragon. Keeping my feet off the slimy bottom, I swam over to the dragon and let the water tumble over my head. On the way there, I saw what appeared to be the only other living thing in the pool. What I thought was the eye of a silver fish turned into a black spot on a leaf that was spiraling to the bottom of the pool.

The water in the middle was deep enough to tread water. I swept my arms in front of me, open and close, open and close. I happened to glance down at the bottom of the pool. The blazing sun overhead, combined with the current created by my moving arms, created a stunning image on the bottom of the pool. I could see the dark shadow of my body, and radiating out from that shape were concentric circles with uneven edges that looked like an aura generated by my body. I felt that these were circles of power created by me but radiating out to the rest of the world, gradually becoming weaker and diffused until the circles were lost in the larger mass of water.

The circle of influence closest to my core was my family. Beyond that was my creativity. Was it possible that through my art and writing this creative force could spread beyond my physical presence? And, like the waving of my arms in the pool, would I have to wave my arms at the world to get noticed?

Mellowed out by my experience alone in the pool, I didn't mind having to wait longer than expected in the parking lot for Nyoman to pick us up to continue our journey.

Chapter Forty-Four

As we drove over one of many mountains on our way to Sanur, which was my final destination in Bali, Nyoman pulled to the side of the road behind a cluster of parked motorcycles. The people from the motorcycles were gathered in front of a temple built into the stone of the mountain.

"I make offering," Nyoman said as he got out of the car.

I'd never seen Suki dressed in a sarong, except for when he took me to the cremation ceremony, or heard him speak about attending any other ceremonies. He seldom talked about how he spent his time away from Double One Villas. He was entirely more loquacious conversing and joking with his friends, sometimes, I wondered, at my expense.

"Why didn't you go with Nyoman to make an offering?" I asked.

Responding as though I'd asked a stupid question, he said, "He make offering for driving."

Just then, a woman approached the front of the car whisking holy water at the windshield and sprinkling flower petals on the hood. As the motorcycle drivers passed our car, I could see some of them had dabs of cooked rice on their foreheads. We were close enough to the temple to see Nyoman, eyes closed and hands clasped in front of his face, as he made his prayer offering at the temple of safe driving. Perhaps making regular offerings at temples like this one was how the Balinese survived the crazy driving in their country. Nyoman had a tiny bit of a red flower stuck behind his ear when he returned to the car.

That was when I remembered something similar stuck behind Suki's ear as I sat close behind him on the motorcycle the previous evening. Maybe he'd attended a ceremony before our outing to the *warung*. At the time I'd thought it was a flower accessory, like jewelry, that he'd worn for our final dinner together.

When Nyoman had settled back in the car, I commented on the practicality of having special temples dedicated to the safety of drivers. His response summed up the philosophy behind the Balinese form of Hinduism.

"God is everywhere."

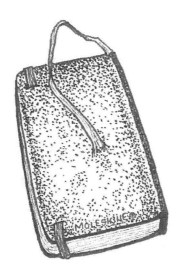

Chapter Forty-Five

The first notebook I used to record my story was a small exquisite Moleskine. In the booklet that came with the notebook, it described the Moleskine as "…the heir and successor to the legendary notebook used by artists and thinkers over the past two centuries: among them Vincent van Gogh, Pablo Picasso, Ernest Hemingway, and Bruce Chatwin. A trusted and handy travel companion, the notebook held invaluable sketches, notes, stories, and ideas that would one day become famous paintings or the pages of beloved books. Today, Moleskine is synonymous with culture, imagination, memory (I can relate especially well to that one), travel, and personal identity." My travel companion came with an excellent pedigree.

The paper was unlined and was a delicate ivory color, pure and unbleached. The cover was cardboard but felt and looked like calf's leather. A pocket was tucked into the back cover perhaps, I romanticized, as a receptacle for a loved one's lock of hair or a lucky four-leaf clover.

The pocket in my Moleskine held only a receipt for a solitary dinner at Café La Wa La that included one "Banana FF Lassy" and one "Coconut Crusted Fish." Elastic attached to the cover held the notebook closed as if to prevent the words inside from spilling out. A slim wisp of ribbon marked the location of a significant passage or the spot where one had left off writing.

The notebook was the size of my hand, but the thin strong paper meant that the book contained enough pages for much writing—even more so since its size encouraged tiny script. The inscription on the first page was: "In case of loss, please return to:" with blank lines for the appropriate information. What made it unique, though, was the next text: "As a reward: $_____." It was only when I'd completely filled it with my small, cramped writing that I acknowledged ownership of both the book and its contents by writing my name, address, phone number and email address. The reward section I left blank. How could I place a value on two weeks of thoughts and experiences? What value did my story have? Was it valuable only to me or would others enjoy sharing my journey?

My second notebook had a cobalt blue cover with text identifying it as a "Sketch Pad for Artists, 5"x7", 100 pages/50 sheets, Acid-free drawing paper, 150 gms, Item #QSP0507, For Sketching & Notes." This notebook was precise and defined. There was still a value to its contents; the paper was acid-free, potentially indestructible. It was much bigger than palm-sized but still fit my criteria of being small enough to fit in my purse. The binding, black coiled-wire, created a convenient spot to keep my pen and allowed the notebook to stay open flat. The heavy cardboard back cover prevented the whole thing from buckling in the humid air.

When I arrived in Sanur, I started a new notebook. It was big, six inches by seven inches, also with a black coiled-wire binding. But this binding was too big to hold my pen without it falling out. Both front and back covers were heavyweight black matte cardboard. It was heavy, substantial and aggressive. It couldn't be slipped into my purse so I had to carry it by hand or leave it behind in my room. It was too big and heavy to carry everywhere with me. However, it was useful when I was writing at meals because I could leave it open on my lap rather than taking up space on the table.

This was a *serious* notebook. The paper inside was bright white and lined like a school notebook. The lower right-hand corner of the heavy book was embossed with the name of a huge Canadian media company. Andrew had given me this notebook just before I left Canada.

"I thought you might be able to use this on your trip, Ma," he said.

Both my children had been supportive when I asked them whether I was being self-indulgent about wanting to travel to Bali.

"You deserve it, they said. "We'll look after Gran."

July 2002

"So, are you here on your own?"

The stocky but athletic middle-aged man had to lean in close in order to be heard over the pounding disco music. The building—vast and built like a barn—was filled with a writhing, noisy mass of mostly young people.

"Uh, well... Do you see that tall young man in the blue t-shirt over there?" I said.

"You mean the one who's been staring at me?" he asked.

"Yeah, he's my son. I'm here with him and my daughter. I think she's gone to bed."

I waved at Andrew to come over.

"Ma, I think you'd better take it easy on the free samples." He gestured to the bottle of Vex, a vodka carbonated drink that was new on the market. "That stuff might taste like Kool-Aid, but it sneaks up on you." He glowered at the guy who seemed to be acting a little too chummy with me.

"It's okay," he said to Andrew. "Your Mom's in safe hands. I'm a cop."

Andrew looked dubious.

I brushed off my son and continued to enjoy the Vex drinks and the company of the friendly police officer. I turned down his invitation to join him in his cabin for another round of drinks and stumbled along the gravel path to the tenting area.

I now regretted that we'd signed up for the early Sunday morning white water rafting trip not knowing about the Saturday night party. I thought that we could enjoy the swimming, volleyball, kayaking and mountain biking on the Saturday and finish off our weekend with the rafting on Sunday. It would leave enough time to make the five-hour drive back to Toronto on Sunday afternoon.

Good, the tent was in the same place we had set it up on Friday night.

"Hey, Alison, I'm home." I didn't want her to think it was a stranger breaking into our tent.

"Mom, what are you doing?" She sounded annoyed.

"I'm trying to come in," I replied.

"Try using the door instead of the window."

"Oh shit!" I tripped on the guy rope stretching from the top of the corner pole to a peg in the ground. I grabbed at the pole to steady myself.

"You're pulling the tent down!" Alison shouted.

"No, no, everything's okay," I assured her.

I finally found the zipper of the door flap and struggled to unzip it. I knew that if I zipped it past the safety pin about half-way up that it would split apart all the way to the top. Our tent had seen better days, but since we seldom used it, it seemed extravagant to buy a new one. I crawled in, closed the zipper behind me, groped for my air mattress and was soon asleep—still dressed—on top of my sleeping bag.

"Ma, it's time to get up. We have to eat breakfast before they take us to the river."

Too early, too many words, too loud. It registered somewhere in my foggy brain that at least Andrew had made it back to the tent sometime after me.

"No, no," I moaned. "I'm not going anywhere." Eating breakfast and white water rafting were the last things I wanted to do. "You and Alison go for breakfast. I'll just stay here for a bit." I dozed off.

"Time to go." Why were they back from breakfast so soon and why was Alison so cheerful?

"I can't… I'm not," I groaned. "You guys go without me."

"No way," Alison insisted. "It was your idea to come on this family-bonding weekend. You're coming with us." She pulled the plug on my air mattress.

The drive in the yellow school bus was brutal. We were bumped up and down on the hard bench seats as the bus bounced over the rough gravel road to the raft launching site. We marched along a narrow path to the river carrying our helmets and life jackets. Neither Alison nor Andrew offered to lighten my load as I dragged behind. Ours was the last group waiting to board one of the big, yellow rubber rafts. The guide did a headcount.

"We've got thirteen people. The extra person will have to sit in the middle without a paddle."

Thirteen, my lucky number — I was born on Friday the thirteenth.

"It's okay, I volunteer." My hand shot up as I said this. I should be able to survive this. All I have to do is hang on. I wasn't as optimistic when the guide described what to do if the raft tipped and threw us all out.

"That's the best part," one of my fellow passengers said. They were all around the same age as my children — early to mid-twenties — and were keen to get started.

At the end of the first set of rapids we were soaked, but the raft had stayed upright as it bucked its way down the rock-strewn chute of foaming rapids.

"Wasn't that great?" Resting his paddle on the side of the raft, Andrew turned to look at me. "Ma, you don't look so good."

"I think I'm going to puke," I whispered through clenched teeth. I didn't know which felt worse — my pounding head or queasy stomach.

Andrew didn't seem as keen to come to my rescue as he had the night before at the party.

CHAPTER FORTY-SIX

The closer we got to Sanur, the more disappointed I became. The coastal land leveled out, and vegetation no longer crept to the side of the road. The shoulders of the road were wide, and the area was semi-industrial. Even the clothing of the motorcycle drivers and passengers had changed. Instead of bare heads, shorts or sarongs and flip-flops, these people were wearing helmets, jackets, jeans and gloves. Most were using scarves or hands to cover their mouths to block out some of the noxious exhaust fumes from the traffic. There were many more trucks and cars on the road compared to in Amed.

I'd been cast out of paradise and was on the road back to real life. The road became a divided, four lane highway. Vehicles had to come to almost a full stop to cross unwieldy changes in the surface of the roadway.

Nyoman's voice jarred me from my dark thoughts.

"You like visit batik workshop? Belong to friend. Half of money for poor people." He knew that I liked local textiles, and he also knew how to play on my social conscience.

"Okay," I said without much enthusiasm.

We pulled through ornate gates into a huge, walled compound with a substantial parking lot, numerous workshop buildings and a large store. It immediately reminded me of arriving at one of the places in China that tourists are taken to, ostensibly for an educational tour of a factory or workshop but inevitably leading to a showroom of products. In China, it had been enamel, jade, pearl, silk and clay workshops.

Two artisans, picturesquely arranged on an outdoor patio, were applying wax onto fabric. An official greeter and guide explained the batik process and then led me to the showroom. He presented me with a complimentary container of water and accompanied me on my tour of the huge textile supermarket. The prices, in American dollars, were hand written on slips of paper.

"Today, everything half price," my guide said.

As P.T. Barnum said, "There's a sucker born every minute," and since I was the only customer, I felt like that sucker. To be fair, the products were beautiful, including clothing for children and adults; pillow covers; cotton and silk scarves and sarongs; and fabric purses, bags and wallets. I succumbed to the subtle attention of my guide/salesman. I bought two pieces of batik fabric, paying for each almost exactly what I paid for my first day's hasty sarong purchase in Ubud.

CHAPTER FORTY-SEVEN

We had not stopped for lunch, and I was getting cranky. Having no reservations for a place to stay made me nervous. The first hotel Nyoman stopped at was a block away from the water. The price was forty-five American dollars a night including breakfast. The room was adequate, but it was available for one night only, not the four that I needed. The three of us all got back into the car. When I saw the barrier and guard house at the entrance of the second place Nyoman chose to turn into, I knew it would be out of my price range. My hunch was confirmed when the receptionist said a room would cost one hundred and twenty-five American dollars a night.

At the third place, there was a gatehouse and a barrier with two guards. One of them used a mirror to check for bombs under the car. Welcome to post-terrorism Bali. The rate for the standard room was sixty dollars a night. Twenty-one percent tax was added and then an additional three percent for paying with a credit card. This hotel was big with forty-five rooms arranged in two-story buildings containing four units each. There was a swimming pool and the hotel was located on the beach.

The room I was shown was on the second floor, huge, nicely decorated with heavy carved furniture, a mini refrigerator, a bathtub, WIFI in the room, a television and air conditioning. The last two amenities I could do without. The balcony was about eight feet wide and twenty feet long with several planters filled with cactus plants with a spiky stem that ended in delicate coral and cream varigated flowers. The unusual flowers, which would be interesting to draw, tipped the balance in my decision to stay. Tired and hungry, I resigned myself to spending almost two and a half times what I'd spent for my lodging in Amed. I didn't want to waste the rest of the day looking for a place to stay.

Back in the lobby, Nyoman was talking with a fellow driver from Amed who had arrived at the hotel with two Canadian women. It dawned on me that this was the hotel Nyoman wanted me to take all along and the first two stops were decoys. When he saw I was staying, he brought a porter over to me.

"My cousin," he said, motioning to the man. "He look after you."

I handed Nyoman what I knew was the standard fare for the trip between Amed and Sanur with a little extra to cover his time for our stops. Possibly, he was also getting a commission from the hotel. From his unsmiling response I could tell that he'd been expecting more, maybe even the full amount of his license renewal fee that he'd casually mentioned during the car ride.

Suki didn't get up from the curb where he was smoking and text messaging on his cell phone. I handed him some money, and he casually put it in the pocket of his jeans.

My disgruntled mood wasn't improved by the dismal, overpriced salad I ordered in the dining pavilion. The lettuce was bitter and wilted and the croutons were moldy. On the way back to my room, I passed a gardener using a noisy, smelly gas lawnmower to cut the grass. Back at Double One Villas the gardener had either used a pair of cutting shears or his hands to accomplish the same task.

CHAPTER FORTY-EIGHT

In Sanur there was a brick paved walkway all along the edge of the beach in front of the hotels. It was partially shaded by trees, and my guide book had suggested that it was a pleasant three-mile bicycle ride or place to stroll. Determined not to have dinner at my hotel, I discovered in a short walk that there was both a soup kitchen slightly off the path and a *warung* located right on the beach adjacent to the path.

I returned to the *warung* later that evening for my solitary dinner in the light of the full moon. I couldn't get a glass of red wine in Amed, so I wanted to celebrate the full moon by ordering one here. Like Amed, they had none in stock. I settled for a small bottle of beer served in a cool, frosty glass. To help me sleep that night, I closed my windows and turned on the air conditioner to keep out both the mosquitoes and the sound of a nearby disco. I did not succumb to the temptation to turn on the television.

Breakfast, included in the price at my hotel, Vila Shanti, was a buffet. At the entrance of the dining pavilion was a sign indicating that guests should check their names on a list. That list proved to be a public source of private information about guests. It showed our room numbers, our name (I was *Mrs.* Livey), date of arrival, date of departure, our nationality and the number of people in our room. By signing opposite all this information, it also indicated to others if we had come in for breakfast. By the second morning, my name had changed to Lively, but I was still a Missus.

I was the only Canadian on the list. The two other Canadian women, who'd also been brought here by a driver from Amed, must have decided that either the price or the room wasn't right. Many of the people on the list were either from Switzerland or Holland with the occasional German or Belgian. Most of the rooms and the tables were occupied by couples.

After checking out the food in the serving trays, I chose a variation of my breakfast at home. I had coffee, papaya juice and sweet black rice pudding topped by yogurt and sliced bananas. The bananas were the size of fingers, and it took two of them to produce a serving.

I saw that the tide was higher than when I'd arrived the previous afternoon when the cove, protected by a reef, was a partially exposed bog of knee-deep water. High tide was the only time to swim and try snorkeling. I donned my gear and went backwards into the water so the flippers wouldn't trip me up. I finned out to a line of buoys hoping that they were markers for pieces of coral and was disappointed when they were not. I'd just about given up hope of seeing any fish or coral and was headed back to the shore when something darted up in front of me. It was a sea snake, the same dull color as the muddy reeds where it had been hiding. I kicked harder with my flippers to get away from it. I found out later that sea snakes are poisonous. I could see why the vendors beside the promenade path were trying to sell snorkeling trips via glass bottom boats to spots outside the reef.

CHAPTER FORTY-NINE

At *Warung Famili.IIM*, the makeshift restaurant where I had noodle soup each day for lunch, I met a kindred soul in the owner, Iim. About my age, she was friendly without being fawning. She, like so many others, asked why I wasn't traveling with my family and/or husband. After I gave the usual explanations, Iim revealed that she also was separated from her husband using the same splitting motion of her hands that I'd used to visually illustrate my marital status.

"Son with husband," she said. She, like other Balinese women, had to leave her child behind when her marriage ended.

Thursday, April 9, 1992

Why I am so unhappy on the weekends is that I miss the children so much. I think I am afraid of losing them—of John charming them away from me. They are such wonderful creatures—thank God for his gift.

Hearing that I was from Canada, she said, "I have customer from Canada. Come here every day. You eat together tomorrow?"

I asked, "Man or woman?"

Iim responded, "Man, but you only eat together."

"Since it's a man, I will definitely come back here for lunch tomorrow!" Was this a wily sales technique to guarantee return business?

There was no written menu at *Warung Famili.IIM* and no chalkboard with a menu either. You had to ask Iim what she'd made that particular day and then select your meal from three choices. The only sign I saw was a small hand-lettered one saying "ginseng coffee," so I returned that afternoon for a coffee break. I sat and enjoyed the sweet beverage while watching whole families arriving on a single motorcycle to spend this holiday at the beach.

The *warung* was located beside one of the few spots that provided public access to the beach. I watched local families and tourists walk and ride bicycles along the promenade. One woman was riding a bicycle with a huge metal pan balanced on her head. I watched a mottled black-and-tan dog with a white-tipped tail and sock feet visit each table hopeful for a handout. I watched as Ana, the owner of the open-fronted shop attached to Iim's *warung*, negotiated with one customer over the price of a fabric bag and with another over the price of a baseball cap. In all my time in Bali, I'd only seen two of the local people wearing baseball caps.

As I sat writing and watching what was happening around me, a woman reached as high as she could to a branch of the tree that sheltered the three tables at the *warung*. She handed something she had picked from the tree to her young daughter. Iim also reached up into the tree and presented me with a sphere the size and appearance of a large gooseberry.

"Eat," she said. "You like."

Rather than being sour and firm like a gooseberry, it was surprisingly sweet and soft.

"What is this called?" I asked.

The word she used sounded like "cherry," but it was unlike any cherry I'd ever sampled because there was no pit.

It had been a pleasant way to spend an afternoon, shaded by the canopy of the mystery fruit tree, observing the busy life around me.

When I was ready to leave, I said to Iim, "How much for the coffee?"

"Five thousand rupiah," she replied.

I was surprised and pleased at the price, which was the equivalent of about fifty-five cents. It was one-quarter of the cost of a plain coffee at Vila Shanti. I had a ten thousand rupiah bill in my hand ready to pay her and waved away the five thousand rupiah bill she offered back as change.

"The money is well worth it considering how long I stayed at your table. I enjoyed my time here. Thank you."

She seemed genuinely pleased.

The tide was out again, and in the hazy glow of the late afternoon light, I watched people wading in the reedy goop. One boy had a starfish in each hand and was wading out of the shallow water where he had found them towards his mother sitting on the beach. A father kicked a soccer ball to his son. A group of about twenty people were sitting in the shade of a large tree enjoying a picnic meal. It seemed to be a typical holiday afternoon; an idyllic scene that could have been anywhere in the world.

I was alone but not lonely.

Returning from a swim in the pool after the pleasant afternoon observing families at the beach, I started organizing my things for the projects I planned to do after dinner. One of those tasks was to continue copying my story from notebook to netbook computer. I hadn't finished transcribing from the second notebook, the cobalt blue artist's sketchbook. I looked around the room for it, at first casually, but with increasing panic when I couldn't find it. Sweat accumulated on my brow, even in the air-conditioned room. I started to chew at the nail on my right index finger, a nervous habit I hadn't regressed to since arriving in Bali. I felt as if part of me had died. I'd lost the middle section of my story, and there was no way I could reconstruct the narrative.

I looked everywhere—on the balcony, in the bathroom and in the wardrobe where I locked away my passport and my netbook when I wasn't using it. I looked in all the drawers in the desk and bedside tables. I looked in my suitcases, my purse, my blue nylon bag and my snorkel equipment bag. I looked under the cushions of all the chairs including those on the balcony. I looked under the bed, under the pillows on the bed and even turned down the heavy bedspread. I had visions of retracing my steps of the last twenty-four hours. I had images of groveling at the reception desk, in the dining room and of going to each of the other forty-four rooms asking, pleading with the people for a sighting of my lost notebook. I knew I hadn't written my name on it. I could picture some Balinese person, having picked it up off the promenade, puzzling over the densely packed pages of words, sentences and sketches trying to fathom the source of this strange artifact. I was bereft and was now shaking from both lack of food and from panic.

About to leave my room to begin the wider search for the precious notebook, I glanced back at the bed. I'd been looking for the distinctive color of the cover, but I'd left the book open at an inside page, folded back on itself. Almost crying with relief, I pounced on the book, unfolded the cover to the front and placed it in the middle of the desk. I was more upset thinking I'd lost that notebook than I would have been at the loss of my passport or wallet. Maybe the full moon did have the power to discombobulate and cause mayhem, especially for those of us who were "moon children."

CHAPTER FIFTY

At one-thirty in the morning, I was regretting having the ginseng coffee so late in the day. Ginseng on its own is a stimulant. Coffee contains caffeine—another stimulant—and the two together, although tasty, carried enough of a wallop to keep me awake most of the night. I normally sleep on my side but tried lying on my back. My arms were flung open, my legs spread apart to try to dissipate the energy coursing through my body. Suddenly, it felt as though someone had sat down on my bed. There was enough ambient light in the room to see that there was no one there. The next sensation was that of shaking, a movement similar to that created by one of those massage beds, found years ago in cheap motels. It dawned on me that I was experiencing an earthquake. Rather than being scared, I waited for more movement. Nothing happened and I fell asleep soon after.

Each day in Sanur, I walked south along the promenade to reach both the *Warung Famili.IIM*, where I had lunch, and the *warung* on the beach, where I ate my dinner. One morning I was curious to see what was along the promenade to the north of the hotel. To my surprise and delight, I discovered a museum that was written up in my guidebook, but I'd despaired of finding. The Le Mayeur Museum was the home and studio of a Belgian artist who came to Bali in 1932 for a planned stay of eight months. Bewitched by both Bali and a fifteen-year-old Balinese dancer, Ni Pollock, he returned the following year to build a house and studio—which I'd just discovered—and ultimately married Ni Pollock. Both at the museum and in the guidebook, there was no mention of a Mrs. Meyeur back home in Belgium.

Ni Pollack, with a few of her dancer friends, became the main subject of Mayeur's work. At that time, some Balinese women went bare-breasted, which was well documented in Meyeur's paintings. The attractive subject matter of beautiful young women in an exotic setting no doubt enhanced the sale of his work back home in Europe. Maybe I should have been making drawings of young, virile Balinese men rather than spending so much of my time writing. I'm sure I would have had no trouble hiring models to pose for me. Unfortunately, figure drawing is not my artistic oeuvre so the results might not have financed a return trip.

The rooms of Le Mayeur's house, modest in size, had walls and window shutters elaborately carved with decorative floral motifs. A built-in wardrobe and unusual corner cupboard, as well as tables, were similarly carved. Two of the outside walls of the house were intricately carved—from stone—and the designs included figures and creatures from Balinese culture. All of the interior swinging doors were painted red, were very narrow and had a high threshold.

The walls of the rooms were crammed with Le Meyeur's paintings, all in dark, carved wood frames. Small landscapes of scenes in Europe were loosely painted in an impressionistic manner, but the colors were dull and murky. This was in contrast to the large, colorful, figurative work done in Bali of Ni Pollack, both alone and in the company of her friends. During the war, due to a lack of traditional art supplies, Le Meyeur painted on either rice sack cloth called *bagor* or on woven reed mats.

I noticed in the visitor's register that the visitor before me on the previous day was also a woman from Canada. We had been the only visitors during those two days.

The Swiss and Dutch guests at Vila Shanti were mostly late middle-aged couples. I didn't feel as bad about my blossoming body every time I saw two women, probably sisters, in bikinis that exposed stick arms and legs with hip and collar bones sharply defined by a lack of natural padding. The only guests to befriend me at the hotel were a tall, elderly Swiss man and his petite, also elderly, wife. She had been born on an island in Northern Indonesia. We met in the dining pavilion where I sometimes went to use the WIFI because the signal was stronger there than on the balcony of my room.

"You're always working," he said. "Either you are writing in a notebook or using your computer."

He was right. Other than a few walks along the promenade or an occasional swim in the pool before dinner, there wasn't much that engaged my departing spirit of adventure. I didn't even feel like swimming in the ocean after my close encounter with the sea snake.

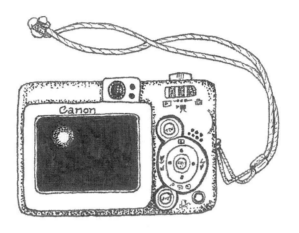

CHAPTER FIFTY-ONE

On my third visit to the beach *warung* to have dinner, the only people there were two young men and a woman, all in their thirties. One of the men had an expensive camera set up on a portable tripod pointing out to the ocean where the full moon was scheduled to make an appearance.

I recognized American accents in the conversation between the two men, so I piped up from my table, "That's a substantial camera. You must be able to take great photos of the moon."

Having broken the ice, we chatted back and forth, and they finally asked me to join them at their table. I initially demurred, not wanting to sacrifice my prime writing time. Quickly realizing how antisocial that was, I accepted their invitation, picked up my notebook and moved to their table.

We exchanged the standard information. Zee, whose full name, Zabrina, meant *desert flower*, and Bart, whose name Barthram, meant *glorious raven*, were brother and sister who were visiting their mother. She was born in Indonesia; their father was from Singapore, and that combination of parental genes had produced attractive children with the dark hair and skin of Indonesia but with facial features that were Caucasian. They had grown up in the United States, and although Bart was an American citizen, Zee had retained her Indonesian citizenship. The third member of their group was Shannon, Zee's boyfriend, from Syracuse, New York. He had been traveling in Southeast Asia for a few months but had now joined Zee and Bart to meet their family and explore Bali together.

Shannon had time to travel between obtaining a Masters of Business Administration degree from George Washington University and the start of a two-year Peace Corps stint in the Republic of Georgia.

"Is Zee going with you to Georgia? I asked.

A significant look was exchanged between them.

Shannon hesitated before answering. "No, as a Peace Corps member, I'm not allowed to have a partner with me. I'm not even allowed visitors for the first four months. We'll be apart for at least a year."

Zee was studiously examining the woven reed placemat on the table as Shannon spoke. I know from experience the hazards of long-distance relationships.

January 21, 2006

Dear Friends,

I would like to share the happy news with you that Bob Skillett and I became engaged on New Years Eve aboard the Norwegian Spirit as it was heading towards the Caribbean. Ours is a very romantic story.

Last March (2005), Mom and I embarked on another one of our "cruises of a lifetime," starting at Sydney, Australia, sailing up the Eastern coast past the Great Barrier Reef, visiting Cairns, Darwin, Singapore, Kuala Lumpur, Viet Nam and Bangkok. On the third night out, Mom and I were just about to get up from dinner when a single gentleman sat down at the next table. Instantly Mom confronted him, "Are you alone?" and when the reply was in the positive she shot back, "So is she!" pointing to me. I was mortified and managed to stammer out, "No I'm not, Mom, I'm with you!" He glanced my way and his first words were,"You're beautiful." With an opening line like that it was hard to resist when he invited me to join him for a drink later in the evening. The bar where we arranged to meet was where Bob had made good friends with a group of Aussies. On his arrival there, he informed them that he had just met a lady in the dining room who was soon to join him. The Aussies thought he was pulling a fast one especially when he didn't know the name of the lady. There were many shocked looks when I strolled up to the bar. Once we knew each other's names, we hit it off and the rest is history.

Ours is truly an international love story. Bob was born in the east end of London, worked in the R.A.F. on bases all over Europe and Asia and has been retired and living on the Mediterranean Island of Cyprus for almost 20 years. Since March, we have traveled to each other's homes twice and met up in England in August where I was warmly welcomed by his late wife Christine's family. A side trip to Prague was magical. Around every corner was beautiful architecture, and we enjoyed listening to both classical music and Dixieland jazz in the evenings. I reintroduced Bob to a bicycle to explore the Waterfront Trail here in Toronto, and he gave me a quick lesson in darts when we joined his fellow Brits in Cyprus.

Our plans for 2006 include me traveling to Cyprus in February, and together we will visit the Maldives (where Bob was once based). We are looking forward to sand, sunshine and snorkeling. I will return home March 1 (where I will be preparing for an exhibition of my work at Open Studio, opening March 9). Tentative plans could include Bob coming to celebrate Mom's 85th Birthday in April and Alison and Gareth's wedding in June. Definite plans are a Baltic Cruise in May where Bob and I will be chaperoned by Andrew, Mom and Bob's friends, Joe and Joyce, from Cyprus. I will be meeting Bob again in September in England for his niece, Sarah's, wedding. As a grand finale to our excellent adventures in 2006 we will be meeting again in November for a land tour in South Africa. In response to my many female friends, no I will NOT share him!!!

I have been blessed with a wonderful life: the excitement and wonder of exploring the world with a loving partner who makes me very happy, balanced by the satisfaction of returning home to my family and work. I have teaching and custom printing jobs waiting for me when I return home, and I am sure the traveling will inspire many new pieces of art-work. Thank you to the many friends who have expressed their happiness for us. We don't know exactly where our adventures will lead us, but we sure are having fun getting there!

Cheers, Lorna

Engaged one New Year's Eve on a Caribbean cruise; disengaged the next New Year's Eve on a cruise to Hawaii.

Shannon and I were both writing about our journeys. Being younger and more computer savvy, his writing was for a blog. I made a conscious decision before my trip that I wouldn't be writing a blog. Although I was emailing installments home to my children and a friend, I wanted my story to be published as a book, something real and concrete. As an artist, my products were tangible objects. As a writer, my product would also be a material object, a book that could be held in the hand, carried on a trip, read in a bathtub (my favorite reading spot) and picked up for a moment or an hour. I wasn't opposed to the words being stored and read in digital form, but I didn't want the fragmentation of a blog.

We talked about the concept of writing for an audience. Yes, we were writing for ourselves, but we also hoped that other people would want to read what we had to say.

"Since I'm writing for an audience," he said, "I try to leave out the trivial details of traveling that might bore my readers. I know that at least two family members, my father and grandmother, are reading my blog because they left comments on my blog page." He smiled wryly.

"Maybe only my family and a few friends will want to read my story," I said. "I'm hoping, though, that it might appeal to a broader audience. Just think, a baby boomer version of Eat, Pray, Love."

"How about the movie version," Shannon said. "Which actor

should play you?"

"Susan Sarandon," I answered confidently.

They agreed enthusiastically with my choice. We had a more difficult time trying to decide who should play Suki.

"Justin Bieber," Bart blurted out.

I snorted in disgust.

CHAPTER FIFTY-TWO

I had come back to my room with a big smile on my face. Not only was I mellowed out by having a glorious massage, but I'd met, not one, but two charming men.

As I approached my regular lunch spot, *Warung Famili.IIM*, I noticed that the one vacant table already had an occupant. Maybe this was the Canadian man Iim had promised. Ana, the proprietor of the shop next to the *warung*, guided me to a spot beside him. We were sitting at the long table usually occupied by a changing group of Swiss, German, Dutch and Scandinavian visitors. Most of them came to Bali for two or three months every year, stayed at the same lodging each time and congregated here in the early afternoon. They had established friendships that were rekindled each time they returned for their long stays. The table where they met was called the international table.

The short but muscular man, who appeared to be in his mid-sixties, was enjoying a cold beer and welcomed me when I sat down. He was from Germany and was staying at an inexpensive homestay nearby for four months. His English was passable and the conversation proceeded slowly. I learned that he too enjoyed snorkeling and was a diver as well. I told him of my disappointment with my snorkeling experience in front of the hotel, and he motioned towards the ocean.

"You must swim past reef," he said.

I looked out to where he was pointing and could barely make out the waves breaking over the reef in the far distance.

"I don't think I should swim that far alone and to take a boat costs thirty dollars for only an hour."

"You have ...?" he said, raising and lowering his arms in a paddling motion because he didn't know the English words for swim fins.

"Yes," I replied, "But it's too far to swim when I don't know the water." In the back of my mind, I was also thinking of my unpleasant encounter with the sea snake.

Gradually, I figured out that he was trying to tell me we could swim out together if I hadn't been leaving the following day. I'd finally found a snorkeling partner, although one who couldn't speak much English, but it was too late in my trip to take advantage of his offer. We were able to communicate well enough to discover that we had both snorkeled in the Maldives. He had stopped going there eleven years ago when the atolls began to be developed with expensive and exclusive resorts for the high-end tourist trade. He had been coming to Bali for ten years to the same homestay for long stays, and he was paying the equivalent of about eleven dollars a night, which included breakfast. He shook his head on hearing what I was paying at my hotel.

"I go to lodging. They have card. I bring for you." He hopped on a bicycle and was gone.

The German man returned with the card, and once again sitting down beside me, he ordered another beer while lighting a cigarette. A new man joined us, sitting in a chair at the end of the long table. He was tall, wore a white, short-sleeved shirt that contrasted nicely with his deep tan and had a large, but neatly trimmed moustache that gave him a distinguished look. A strong aquiline nose made him look like the captain of a Greek fishing boat. He greeted everyone in a way that indicated that he was one of the regulars. He turned to me with a smile and asked me something in Dutch.

"I'm sorry," I said, "I don't speak Dutch."

"Then I will have to talk to you in your language," he said in fluent English.

He asked the expected first question of all travelers, "Where are you from?"

"I'm from Canada. Toronto," I said.

"I have visited Vancouver. I have also stayed in Niagara Falls. I waved in the direction of Toronto across the lake." He seemed to be trying to impress me with his travels in Canada.

"There are many Portuguese in Toronto, are there not?"

"There are people from all over the world in Toronto," I answered.

He was a Belgian citizen but since he now lived in Portugal, he knew that many people emigrated from there to Canada.

I turned to my German seat mate, not wanting him to feel left out of the conversation. I asked him his name.

"Hartmut," he said. "Old German name."

The Belgian man added, "It means *a heart with a lot of courage*."

Hartmut asked me my name.

"Lorna," I said.

He looked puzzled and asked me to write it down on his cigarette package.

"Not common," he said.

"It was invented by an English novelist, Richard Blackmore, as the name of his heroine, Lorna Doone," I said.

I didn't explain to the men the more accurate account of why I received my name. The first child born to my parents was a girl, Christine, and it was hoped their second child would be a boy. They had even picked out a name. I was to be Lawrence Arthur, Junior. My father was most often called Lorne, and so when I was born, Lorna was chosen, a feminine approximation of his name. Growing up, I was somewhat of a tomboy and tried in many ways to be the son my parents never had.

The tall Belgian looked at me with a twinkle in his eye. "So, Lorna from Canada, do you not want to know my name?"

He was Andre.

"That's the same name as my son, Andrew," I said.

"You have excellent taste," he responded.

Before he arrived, I'd finished my soup and Iim had removed the empty bowl. I was waiting for Ana to return from placing offering baskets at several nearby temples. The previous day, she had talked me into having a massage in the back of her small shop. I had enough money left to indulge in one last massage.

Andre ordered *mi goreng*, one of the three dishes offered daily at the *warung*. Turning to me, he asked gallantly, "Aren't you going to have something to eat?"

"I've already eaten my noodle soup. I come here every day for lunch."

"And where do you have your dinner?" he asked.

"Back over there, along the promenade, is a *warung* with tables right on the beach. Their fish is wonderful and the price is right. Like here," I added.

"I had a splendid dinner last night at a hotel next to the one where I'm staying. They had a live band with a singer. She was really quite good," he said.

"I heard some music last night. It seemed to be coming from somewhere near my hotel."

"Where are you staying?" he asked.

"Vila Shanti," I answered,

He put out his hand. "Welcome neighbor," he said. "Would you like to have dinner with me tonight?"

"Yes, that would be lovely," I responded without hesitation.

Hartmut looked a bit crestfallen at this turn of events.

"I'll drop by to see your homestay on the way back to my hotel." I didn't want him to feel left out.

Ana was ready for my massage.

"I would massage you for free," Andre said.

"You should pay *me* for the privilege of massaging my body," I shot back.

I left the two men chatting with each other. Ana pulled a rack of clothing across the front of her shop, motioning that I should get undressed and lie down on the hastily assembled table. I did as I was told, and just as I lay face down wearing only panties, Hartmut looked over the clothing rack to bid me adieu.

I kept my promise to Hartmut to visit his homestay. It was the first time I'd ventured up to the main road, but the place wasn't hard to find. Hartmut was sitting in front, at the restaurant attached to the homestay, and was having another beer with a Balinese friend. His face lit up when he saw me. As I went to join them at the table, I noticed Andre had just turned onto the main road on a bicycle, and I gave him a friendly wave as he rode past.

I'd come to look at the rooms at the homestay to see if they would be appropriate on a future visit. I was also curious to see what was offered for such a cheap price.

"Hartmut, do you think someone could show me a room?" I asked.

He disappeared for several minutes.

"Come, I show you my room. Then owner show you new one." He led the way up a flight of stairs. I felt no threat of danger following a man I'd just met to his room.

Hartmut's room was serviceable and pleasant, a step up from my first room at Jati Homestay in Ubud. The new room, although not as large and posh as the room at my hotel, was clean and bright. The small courtyard was cluttered with construction debris.

"Owner make nice garden soon. Many flowers," Hartmut explained.

The homestay was beside the noisy road and not on the beach, but it was also one-sixth of the cost of my hotel.

As we parted, Hartmut put out his hand.

"I have gift for you," he said.

When we shook hands, I felt a cool, smooth shape left behind in my palm. It was a polished heart-shaped stone with the words "VIEL GLÜCK" printed on in red magic marker. "Check words at home," he said.

On my last full day in Bali, I'd received a heart from a man whose name meant "a heart with a lot of courage" and an invitation to dinner with a man named Andre.

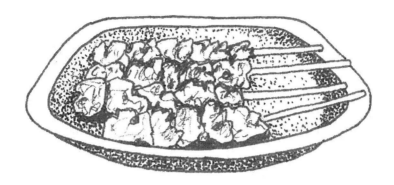

CHAPTER FIFTY-THREE

I was down to my last few hours in Bali. Packing was easy since I hadn't emptied my suitcase when I arrived in Sanur four days before. It was my last opportunity to go for a swim in the ocean. I lay floating in the salt water, being lifted up and down, up and down in the gentle swell. I flung my arms wide open and closed my eyes to block out the glaring rays of the sun. I tried to relax every muscle in my body, to give it over to the supporting mantle of water.

I thought about what to wear for my big date. The choices were narrow considering that most of my clothes were dirty. In Amed, I washed my clothing as needed, mostly t-shirts and underwear. I used the backpacker's technique of doing laundry. While I was taking a shower, I would throw the dirty clothes on the floor of the shower. As I shampooed my hair and soaped up my body, the suds would fall onto the dirty clothing. I would stomp my feet as I washed. My technique was similar to that of stomping grapes in the old fashioned way to extract juice to make wine. Towards the end of the shower, I would pick up each item and rigorously rub it against itself to scrub away the dirt. As I rinsed my body under the water, I also held the clothing up, piece by piece, to rinse away the soapy water. Wringing out as much water as I could was important because the humidity was so high in Bali that it took forever for the clothes to dry, especially the t-shirts. Those I hung over the railing on my porch. I tried to be more discrete with the panties, either hanging them from some cross bars of the table on the porch or draping them over a wicker basket. I had thoughts of festooning the bushes around my bungalow with my wet laundry to expose it to the sun like I'd seen in the family compounds, but I realized that this could put off potential customers at Double One Villas. They might not be impressed by a tawdry display of oversized t-shirts and panties blooming from the garden plants.

I had to decide between the one dress I'd brought with me or a pair of still presentable beige pants. I could pair the pants with a beaded, brown top that was a pass-me-down from my daughter. The unworn dress was perhaps too flamboyant. The pattern on the fabric was similar to that of a leopard, which might convey the wrong image to my date. Besides, being sleeveless the dress did nothing to camouflage my batwing arms.

The cotton pants were lightweight, and the long pant legs would cover mosquito target areas. More importantly, they had an expandable waistband. From the bottom of my suitcase, where they had languished for a month, I unearthed my pair of dressy sandals. Although I'd had them for two years, they were still in style and hadn't been used as wading shoes. I also excavated a black, push-up bra and (semi) matching panties from the mass of otherwise dirty clothes in my suitcase. The bra presented a dilemma: support and enhancement over droopy and comfortable, which until now had been my choice throughout the trip. I decided that I could survive the torture of up-and-perky for one evening. The black panties might show through the thin cotton pants, but diminished evening light would work in my favor.

I showered, deciding that defoliation of a month's worth of hair under my arms and on my legs was necessary. For the first time during my trip, I applied eye shadow, mascara, lipstick, hair pomade and cologne, rationalizing that since I'd lugged them all the way from Canada, I may as well use them. I took a swig from the miniature bottle of mouth wash that hadn't been cracked open. Being practical, I sprayed my bare arms and ankles with mosquito repellent, hoping the scent was complementary to my cologne. Suitably clothed, spritzed, defuzzed and embellished, I left to meet my date in the reception area of our hotel.

Andre was casually but elegantly dressed in light pants and a short sleeved shirt. He commented on my punctuality but not on my appearance. I left the choice of dining venue up to him since he'd already been in Sanur for two weeks.

"There is a good restaurant nearby. The owners are from Belgium so I have eaten there often," he said.

He skillfully took my elbow to maneuver me across the motorcycle raceway that doubled as a street. I had the tendency of looking in the wrong direction when crossing streets because the Balinese drove on the left side of the road when they weren't competing for the middle.

As we were about to turn into the laneway leading to the restaurant, the lights went out. I was no longer surprised by electricity failures, this being the fourth one in a month's time. We headed towards a couple of spots of light in the distance finding out that they were flashlights being held by the restaurant's staff. In the dim light, I recognized two other couples standing at the bar who earlier in the day had been at the international table of Iim's *warung*. They greeted Andre, and I was ignored except for a sharp scrutinization by the women. They talked animatedly in either German or Dutch. Andre had told me he was fluent in Dutch, German, French and English and semi-fluent in Portuguese and Italian. Finally, noticing my lack of participation in the conversation, one of the men switched briefly to English.

We could see a few lights coming on at places that had power generators.

"We will go to another restaurant," Andre said. "The owner has told me he has no motor."

Just as he finished saying this, the lights flashed back on. The light flooded a large outdoor dining space partially protected by a roof. It was much fancier than the *warungs* I'd been eating at with table linens and candles, rather than woven cane placemats and cutlery wrapped in paper napkins. A female singer and two guitarists provided pleasant background music.

"What would you like to drink?" Andre paused as he looked at the menu. "My, the bottles of wine are rather expensive." Shouldn't he have known that if he had already eaten there?

I took this as a clue that ordering wine would be an extravagance. I made do with a small bottle of the local beer, *Bintang*, which I'd already had several times as a dinner beverage.

Perusing the menu, Andre said, "I've wanted to try the *Rijsstaffel*, but it's for two people. Would you like to share it with me? It has many small dishes of food."

It sounded like the Indonesian equivalent of the Spanish *tapas* or Cypriot *meze*. The opportunity to share a variety of dishes sounded tempting.

"That would be lovely," I replied.

The waitress placed many small dishes of food on the table.

"What is this food?" Andre asked her.

She described the contents of each dish.

Gesturing, he said to the server, "This chicken, this chicken and this chicken. Too much chicken."

She said she would consult with the chef and returned to report that pork satay would be added for more variety. The satay arrived coated with a sauce.

"What is this?" he demanded.

"Pork, sir, with a peanut sauce."

"I detest peanuts. I must have ones without sauce." He motioned to the plate, "These will be all for you."

I was glad to oblige as I happened to love peanut sauce. Andre's imperious personality was starting to annoy me. The food resources available to the Balinese were limited, and I'd been happy to be flexible as far as food selection went. My silent, but stress-free dinners with Suki, were beginning to look idyllic compared to this one.

My earlier romantic notions of having met a sophisticated and charming European man were being shattered by his demanding attitude. Granted, his stories of having traveled the world, first as a cruise director on a ship and later through his work in the travel industry, were interesting. We exchanged information about several of our travel destinations. I volunteered details about my relationship status, but he was evasive about his. Finally, with some prodding, he revealed that he lived with a woman in Portugal.

"It's convenient to live together. I can travel without her when I want, and she is happy at home with her friends and her dogs."

My initial enthusiasm about my dining companion had dampened, but it was totally extinguished, like the lights had been earlier, by the arrival of the bill.

From politeness more than anything, I said, "Shall I pay half?"

"Of course," he said without any hesitation.

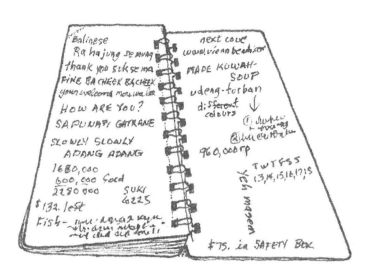

Chapter Fifty-Four

I didn't really expect to hear from Suki once I'd left Amed so I was delighted to receive two emails from him before I left Bali to return home. It meant that I wasn't entirely forgotten and also that my teaching him how to use email was successful.

His messages were brief but poignant. They showed remarkable courage in trying to write to me in my language.

HAI MAM WHAT ARE DOING NOW? IM TRAY THE IMAIL ELON.IM SORY IM RITE NOT SO GOD. I HOPE YOU LIKE STAY THERE

His attempt at spelling the words the way they sounded reminded me of my own laborious task of trying to learn his language. In the back of my second notebook was a record of my own struggles with a foreign language. Eko had helpfully written down the Balinese words for "How are you?" *Sapunapi Gatrane.* My written phonetic version of what I heard was: SAP POON A PE GAT TRANE, printed all in capital letters, just as Suki had done in his email. I'd been cocky thinking I'd learned to say "good morning" really fast and skillfully with the aid of my guide book. For at least four days at Double One Villas, I'd confidently wished all the staff "*selemat pagee*" each morning and was slightly puzzled when they didn't respond. Finally, one of them was brave enough to point out that I was wishing them "good morning" in the Indonesian language, not in their native Balinese. My Balinese version of "good morning" was: RA HA JUNG SE MUNG. They taught me how to say "*adang, adang,*" which meant "slowly, slowly" because that was the speed at which I was learning their language. I was always glad to have my notebook with me so I could refresh my dismal memory before I attempted to say the words.

My response to Suki's first email encouraged him to keep writing.

Hello Suki

I was really happy to get an email from my Balinese son. My Canadian son has been bad because he has not sent me any emails. I really miss Amed and the people there like you. I tried to snorkel in front of the hotel today and all I saw was a sea snake, no beautiful fish or coral like in Amed. I am still doing lots of my writing. I also have been swimming in the swimming pool.

Thank you for showing me so many beautiful things, the fish, the coral, the waterfall, the holy water spring and all the beautiful landscape.

Keep practicing sending emails. You will get better every time.

From your Canadian mother, Lorna

His response was:

helo mam, im reading olready you email. thanks for evriting. but now my job stil lose. becaose you olready life from. now i will salle my motor bike.

I replied:

Dear Suki

I am now at home in Canada. There was a big snow storm here the day before I arrived. The ground is covered with snow. It is very cold here and I have to wear a heavy coat, a hat and warm gloves when I go outside.

I like the weather much better in Bali. Your country is very beautiful and you must be very proud of it.

Thank you for taking me to see so many beautiful things. I hope you have found more customers so that you do not have to sell your motorcycle.

Send me an email. I would like to hear from you again.

Your mother in Canada, Lorna

Chapter Fifty-Five

As I came towards my daughter in the arrivals hall at the airport, she exclaimed, "Mom, you look great. You look at least ten years younger!" With that comment, she stroked the skin on my cheek. "Your skin is so soft."

Now I had confirmation that the water Suki collected in a plastic water bottle from the holy water spring was indeed the elixir of youth. I'd been splashing it on my face every morning for about a week, thinking that it could do no harm. I decanted the remaining water to a smaller water bottle, sealed it in not one, but two plastic bags and packed it in my suitcase. I hoped it had survived the workouts of the baggage handlers in Bali, Taipei and Toronto. I'd intended to present it as a souvenir gift to my almost ninety-year-old mother but was having second thoughts about being so generous. At least one of my goals had been accomplished—that of postponing the march of time towards my dreaded sixtieth birthday.

The second of my goals wasn't as successfully reached—that of making art during my trip. That goal had been sacrificed in the competition for time and attention to my third goal—writing. Granted, I had completed five small painting/drawings but not enough to have justified filling half my suitcase with art supplies.

During my trip, I'd discovered at least two advantages to being a writer rather than an artist. It was much easier to write in public than it was to make art in public. A notebook and a pen are very portable compared to the paper, paints, brushes and assorted paraphernalia required to produce visual art. An errant squirt of juice from the lime I squeezed on my breakfast pancake couldn't do too much harm to my notebook but would probably not have enhanced a drawing. I didn't have critics hanging over me trying to read my words. Attempting to make art in the relative privacy of my porch at Double One Villas attracted the attention of passing staff who came to see what the crazy lady in bungalow six was doing with all the leaves she had gathered from the garden.

I even compromised my plan to loosen up my art. Instead, I painted a very tight watercolor of the view from my porch as if to prove to the staff that I was a real artist. That proof was probably not necessary because in Bali art was so much a part of everyday life.

The second advantage of writing over making art was the storage of the end product. My studio was overflowing with artwork made over a thirty-five year period along with equipment, tools and materials. My writing output in Bali occupied only three notebooks and used up only two ballpoint pens, both of which were liberated from cruise ships. When transcribed into my netbook, they occupied no physical space at all.

The journey I embarked upon was both a physical one and an interior one. Through it, I confirmed my ability to delight in the beauties of nature, both on the land and in the ocean. I was capable of interacting in a positive way with new people, especially those whose culture was so different from my own. More importantly, it taught me to value my own self-sufficiency. And I learned I could live without red wine with dinner and dark chocolate.

Tuesday, April 21, 1992

Feel more positive today. Washed and waxed floor. Realization that John is really very ordinary and I have the potential to be extraordinary without him—to live with my own value systems, to be outrageous or not, to be poor, to be unconventional, to be anything other than the wife of a civil servant. I can be myself and invent myself as I go along. I can do odd jobs, make t-shirts, do house portraits, anything but what he expected of me. I am an artist—I am different, and I will celebrate that difference whether it is through wearing weird clothes or an unorthodox way of making money.

I feel good about myself. I can be eccentric, drive an old car, have grey or orange hair, be introverted or extroverted, quiet or noisy. My children are my treasures and they have a vibrant, loving and wacky mother. I am loved and I am worth it.

The trip to Bali took one month. My life journey began sixty years ago. Without realizing it until I wrote this story, I'd written directions for that journey in my notebook nineteen years earlier on Tuesday, April 21, 1992.

The road ahead beckons with promises of adventure and more un-expected twists and turns.

Bali

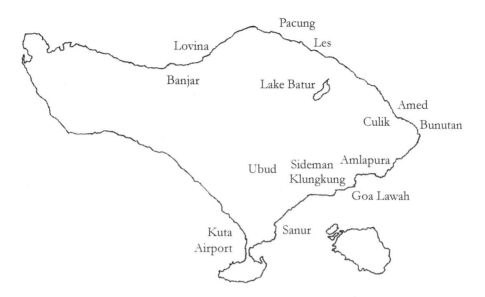

Amed & Bunutan
Double One Villas
Japanese Shipwreck
Pondok Vienna Beach
Wawa Wewe II

Amlapura
ATM machine
Tirta Gangga

Banjar
Air Panas (hot springs)

Culik
Ogoh-ogoh procession

Goa Lawah
Bat Cave Temple

Klungkung

Kuta

Lake Batur
Eco-cultural Bike Tour

Les
Waterfall

Lovina

Pacung
Surya Indigo Workshop

Sanur
Batik Workshop
Le Mayeur Museum
Vila Shanti
Warung Famili.IIM

Sideman
Songket textiles

Ubud
Elephant Cave
Gusti's Garden Bungalow
Jati's Homestay
Monkey Sanctuary
Rice Field Walk
Taksu Spa and Restaurant
Ubud Botanic Garden

ACKNOWLEDGEMENTS

There are many people I want to thank for helping with this book:

Jenny, Marilee and Judi for reading and commenting on drafts of the manuscript;

Jessica for her skill in pointing out unnecessary words;

Greg for his suggestion of a subtitle and superb photography;

Antanas for pointing me in the right direction;

Nicole for her intriguing cover design;

Alison for encouraging me to write the back stories and pointing out ways to improve the book;

Andrew for being willing to share parts of his story and for his creative design work;

Bob for patiently reading many drafts, for his editing skills and steadfast encouragement.

.